Life B

Life B

OVERCOMING
DOUBLE
DEPRESSION

A Memoir

Bethanne Patrick

Counterpoint
Berkeley

First Counterpoint edition: 2023

Library of Congress Cataloging-in-Publication Data
Names: Patrick, Bethanne Kelly, author.
Title: Life B : overcoming double depression : a memoir / Bethanne Patrick.
Description: First Counterpoint Edition. | Berkeley : Counterpoint, 2023.
Identifiers: LCCN 2022057056 | ISBN 9781640091290 (hardcover) | ISBN 9781640091306 (ebook)
Subjects: LCSH: Patrick, Bethanne Kelly—Mental health. | Depressed persons—United States—Biography. | Depression in women—Anecdotes.
Classification: LCC RC537 .P384 2023 | DDC 616.85/270082—dc23/eng/20221214
LC record available at https://lccn.loc.gov/2022057056

Jacket design by Dana Li
Jacket images of plant © name_gravity / Unsplash, roots © Mila Tovar / Unsplash
Book design by Laura Berry

COUNTERPOINT
2560 Ninth Street, Suite 318
Berkeley, CA 94710
www.counterpointpress.com

Printed in the United States of America

10 9 8 7 6 5 4 3 2 1

For my daughters

I was so scared to give up depression, fearing that somehow the worst part of me was actually all of me.

—ELIZABETH WURTZEL

Contents

Introduction

I WILL ALWAYS BE DEPRESSED, AND I'M OKAY WITH THAT

MY HUSBAND WAS UPSET ABOUT DRIVING ME TO THE psychiatric hospital.

"You know you don't need this, right, Beth?" he said, glancing at me from behind the steering wheel of our Jeep SUV. "We can just go home. We can call and tell them you don't need to be admitted."

It was raining. The nighttime northern Virginia roads looked like black ribbons, the kind widows once used to trim mourning gowns. I was so tired from arguing with my husband about whether or not I should enter the hospital.

I was longing for safety. From myself.

"Thanks," I told him. "But I need to go."

———

Two nights earlier I had shaken our house with my sobs, locked in a battle between staying alive and reaching for the assortment of pills, opiates and others, that lined the top of my nearby dresser. They were meant to help me recuperate from recent ankle surgery, after accidentally tripping and falling down our front steps. I wanted to take the pills. If I could just be brave enough to get up and take enough of them, I could be free. Between crying bouts, I checked to make sure they were still there.

They were. Even though I could take them at any time, they remained in the bottles. My husband did not remove them from my dresser. He lay next to me, immobile. Did he believe I wouldn't dare?

When I awoke the next day, dehydrated from all the crying, I called my psychiatrist. She had been urging me to consider in-patient treatment.

"I need to go to the hospital," I said. "I'm not safe. I'm thinking about suicide, and it's not just a cry for help. I want to die."

She lost no time in calling around for a bed. The nearest available was at a private psychiatric hospital. I asked her if I could think about it, and she strongly urged me to get there quickly.

At the time I decided to enter the hospital, I'd been seeing Dr. Chasen for five years. I met with her once a week for talk therapy combined with medication maintenance. I'd chosen her because of her location, an easy drive with ample available parking (these can be big issues for me).

Dr. Chasen did not accept our insurance. I had to pay her in full at the end of each session. Although I had salaried jobs during the years I saw her, Adam was infuriated with each month's bill. "This is such a waste of money!" he would say. "Why can't you find someone within our network?"

He wasn't wrong. If this had been a dentist or a pediatrician or an optometrist, I might have been able to take action. But I was afraid to leave her care after I'd already invested so much time and effort in sharing my psychiatric history with her. After years of moving and switching practitioners, of filling out paperwork, I needed to minimize more changes.

A few hours passed. She called back to find out what I'd decided and wound up speaking to my husband. I was lying in bed again, exhausted.

"She doesn't need to go to the hospital anymore!" he shouted into the receiver. "The real crisis was yesterday!"

I could hear my doctor, her voice so loud it came through the phone speaker clearly. "I'm trying to save your wife's life!" she said. "Don't you understand that?"

Their interaction made me feel numb. Who was right: the person who loved me best, or the professional who knew my disease best?

I couldn't figure out the answer, so I did something else. I called my priest.

When our family manages to attend church, we are Episcopalian. We refer to our clergy as priests. Father Tim came over that afternoon and spoke quietly with me as I sat in my wheelchair, my leg, in a cast, sticking straight out in front of me. He reminded me that asking for help is a sign of strength, not weakness, and that only I could make the decision to do so.

He recalled me to myself, to the fact that I had the power to choose living over dying.

I left a message for my psychiatrist and said I was ready to be admitted.

———

I always understood that we all require support to get through our lives, and sometimes I had a say in that support, and sometimes I did not.

I grew up with a mother who controlled her children's lives because once upon a time she'd wanted that control in her poverty-stricken childhood and didn't get it. I married early, six months after graduating from college, in part because my mother was desperate to see me safe and secure. She understood that I would be taken care of, and we both knew that I needed to be taken care of, because I was emotionally unstable.

So why didn't Adam want to help me?

He was there as I sobbed that I wanted to die. Even a person who did not love his spouse—and he did, and does, love me—would understand that something was wrong.

However, Adam didn't think psychiatric treatment would help me. I'd been seeing psychiatrists for over twenty years, with very little effect. I'd been downing Prozac, Lexapro, Wellbutrin, trying to be compliant, and still there I was, low in mood.

At one point I asked my best friend, "Will I ever be happy?" Because I wasn't. And nothing—not a stable income, not a dream job, not a beloved family, not a yearly vacation by the ocean, not a coterie of supportive friends—nothing made me happy.

Adam had a front-row seat for the Nothing Makes Bethanne Happy performance, which ran, for him, day and night. I understood why he might be reluctant to believe that anything was going to change, that I was ever going to get better.

But now I was actively suicidal. Did he think that as long as he was by my side, nothing bad could happen? That as long as I was hampered by a knee-to-ankle cast, I couldn't find a way to end my life? Sometimes I think that he believed I'd lost the ability to make even that decision. That there was something so wrong with me I wouldn't even be able to choose suicide.

When Adam told me, "You know you don't need to do this," he believed I was past the point of danger, that I'd somehow cried it all out and wouldn't take further action to harm myself. He is trained, as a soldier and a leader, to respond to crises. Doctors are trained to keep patients alive; when their patients die, there is nothing left for them to do. Soldiers respond to danger, and when danger has passed, they move on, mentally on patrol for what comes next.

Adam had kept me safe during the crisis. He had stayed beside me. If I'd managed to reach those bottles, I know he would have pried them from my hands, done everything he could to keep me from swallowing the deadly pills. His upbringing, education, career, and temperament mean he is prepared for the worst and habituated to the best.

But nearly thirty years into our marriage, he still wasn't prepared for my worst, for a disease that rarely abated and never disappeared.

————

When you're admitted to a locked psychiatric ward, anything you bring has to be examined. Goodbye tweezers, spray bottles, clothing with drawstrings. I was allowed the huge bag of books I lugged with me. Those books, which I stacked spines out on the desk next to my single bed, were my bulwark against forgetfulness. I did not want to forget who I was: a reader.

I wasn't yet a writer. I wanted to be a writer. But I wasn't. I wasn't writing. Yes, occasionally I wrote blog posts and articles and book reviews, but often they weren't good. Because I wasn't writing every day. I wasn't practicing the sustained, daily work that is the foundation of an artistic life, of many kinds of lives really.

But I knew I was a reader. I could read for hours and hours, even if I wasn't writing at all. Reading allowed me to sustain a professional identity. I was saying to the other patients, "Look at me, I know who I am. I have not forgotten. I am not as lost as you are." I was a show-off, even at my rock-bottom worst.

I was placed in the suicide-watch room right in front of the nurses' station. That was the biggest division on the ward, between depressives and others, and my first indication that my stay would not be quiet. The door to the room I shared with two other women was only allowed to be closed at night, once bed checks were complete. At all other times the harsh hallway lights and many sounds of other patients kept me from sleep, the only thing I wanted to do.

One man stood at the doorjamb repeating, "Can I get a smoke can I get a smoke can I get a smoke can I get a smoke can I get a smoke," tunelessly and frequently. I lay on my right side and stared at the irregular wall, sometimes counting the bumps until I could fall asleep again. Because I still needed a wheelchair—I found using crutches to get around, given my broken ankle, too unstable—I wasn't required to leave the room and participate in group activities. I was glad, afraid talking to strangers might depress me further.

When I was interviewed by the psychiatrist on call, I was able to sincerely say that my pull toward suicide had passed. We talked for a long time, so long that the nurse served me lunch while we spoke. "It's taco salad day!" she said. "And Friday. That means you can have a Diet Pepsi if you want." I did want, after forty-eight-plus hours of no caffeine. And the taco salad tasted, if not heavenly, at least something like life.

My husband, a stalwart caregiver, showed up for the visiting hours, our younger daughter in tow. I felt terrible that she had to see me in a room where the chairs and tables were bolted to the floor, where I had to be wheeled out to see my family. The usual questions seemed useless. How was your day at school? Do you have any homework due? Is there a soccer game on Saturday? Her father knew the answers already. I didn't. If I did, what was I going to do about them?

Doing something about those answers meant leaving the hospital. Which I did, two days later.

But leaving the hospital didn't mean recovering. That was four years in the future. Four very long years in which I tried and tried and tried to loosen myself from the abyss. Has anyone ever detailed all the things depression has taken away from her? A person "has depression," as if it's added on, when in truth depression is a lack. Better: a lacuna, a void into which all of life's positives disappear.

I'd like to tell you that making changes—moving house, getting more exercise, changing my habits about work—changed my life. The truth is, what changed my life was seeking different medical care. My husband Adam still does not believe in therapy, either for himself, or for me in the long term. It doesn't matter. I make sure I take the meds each morning and night. I love Adam, but if he won't get me to the hospital when I need to go, I have learned that I will get there myself.

———

I have a form of mental illness known as double depression, in which chronic depression spirals into major depressive episodes during times of great stress. As my doctor has explained it, from my earliest experience I've begun each day lower than what we might call normal. And sometimes much lower. On my best days, before I was diagnosed with this condition—which wasn't until age fifty-two—I was depressed. On my worst days I considered ending my life.

I no longer mind talking about depression. Not anymore.

Not that I didn't talk about the state of being depressed, a lot, for many years. I was quite articulate, as one friend recently told me, about my misery.

But being articulate about misery is not the same thing as being open about living with mental illness.

I tried to do anything to hide being mentally ill, even as I regaled friends and colleagues with tales of my anguish, my moods, my misguided attempts to soothe myself. I was ashamed of being different, so I tried to turn my deep sadness into performance art, the performance perhaps titled "I'm Just Like You, Only Sadder."

When you're sad all the time, people who aren't sad fascinate you. How do they do it? How is it possible that they are doing the same things you're doing—going to school, attending Girl Scout meetings, shopping for groceries—but doing those things with happiness, sometimes even joy? Can't they see the futility of it all? Why do they seem content, while you are on the verge of tears?

In my early adolescence, a fog descended. I had been warned about teenage moodiness, but the fog I experienced was less of a cyclical storm and more of a permanent haze. A window seemed to separate me from everyone else, to separate me from genuine smiles and enthusiasm for kickball or shopping or acing tests. My days were cloudy and contained.

I told my mother how miserable I was, how much more miserable I was getting. While she was sympathetic, her own poverty-stricken upbringing made my life seem luxurious. I ate regular meals and lounged in front of the TV; at the same age, she had prepared meager suppers for her siblings. If I was sad and maladjusted, at least I wasn't hungry and cold and frightened. So what if I stayed in my room for hours, alternately sleeping and weeping? "Go outside and get some fresh air," she told me. She meant well, but she had no vocabulary for depression. "Those kids who don't like you are just jealous," she said. "Ignore them." I was a good girl, so I tried.

But ignoring your classmates can make you pretty lonely, and my mind urged a crueler kind of loneliness, the kind that made me stop engaging with the world.

Depression has plagued me ever since.

This is not an exaggeration. Since childhood, I have suffered, to some degree or another, from depression. I should make that plural: depressions. Not because there has been more than one period of time during which I was acutely depressed, although that is true—but because in 2016, I finally received a correct diagnosis: double depression. *The Diagnostic and Statistical Manual of Mental Disorders, Fifth Edition*, or *DSM-5*, defines double depression as the combination of persistent depressive disorder (PDD, what was once known as dysthymia)—a chronic depression that exists most days for a period of two years—and major depressive disorder (MDD). MDD is what we've long called clinical depression, the kind when a person cannot function and loses all hope. (The bullet points of hopelessness encompass staying in bed, eating too much or not eating at all, poor attention to personal hygiene, and so on.)

The concept of double depression has been around since the early 1980s, but the combined terminology—PDD and MDD—is a new addition to *DSM-5*. Double depression is now recognized as a syndrome with distinctive characteristics.

What all this boiled down to for me was bad days, bad days, bad days, and some worse days. On a very good day, I brushed my teeth without thinking about it. On a very bad day, I didn't get out of bed, let alone bother with brushing my teeth. Most of the in-between days involved a long and precise internal monologue: "You need to brush your teeth. Remember to brush your teeth. Get up and move toward the bathroom. All right, you can stay in bed for a few more minutes, but then you have to brush your teeth." It went on and on and on.

Although my mother's tactics did not cure my depression, they did keep my grades up and my schedule packed, so I made it into a top-tier college. But once there, without her support, I lapsed into melancholia, skipped classes, and developed agoraphobic tendencies. I hated leaving my room for anything: library, classes, activities. If the dining room hadn't been just downstairs, I might have subsisted on whatever I could stash in my mini fridge. I managed, somehow, to graduate. I also managed to meet the man who is still my spouse today. But my persistent depression did not lift.

My depression worsened while my husband went to law school and I pursued a master's degree in English. Chalk it up to the pressures of my program, getting older, or the challenges of maintaining a relationship—whatever it was, I couldn't speak articulately in seminars, nor could I make sense of anything I read. "Just work harder," said classmates, hurrying to the library. "Why not have a baby?" asked nonacademic friends. "Why do you cry all the time?" my husband asked.

One afternoon, after hours spent sobbing on our hand-me-down sofa, I had a tenuous thought.

Maybe this was not normal. Maybe I needed some help.

———

I chose a therapist from the Yellow Pages because I liked her name, and I got lucky—I liked her too. I told her about the hopeless thoughts filling my head. She placed her hand on my knee. "You don't have to feel like this," she said. "We might want to consider medication." In that moment, something deep inside me responded, something I had forgotten. The possibility of change set me floating, wondering what it might be like if I wanted to participate in life.

Two weeks later, after dutifully downing a green-and-white capsule daily with my coffee, I woke up and knew something had shifted. It was as distinct as the moment when the optometrist clicks two lenses into place and you can suddenly read everything on the chart. "Which is better?" says the optometrist. "A, or B?" If she took one of those lenses away, I would have Life A. Life A is blurry, fuzzy, difficult to decipher. When she puts it back into place, I have Life B. Life B is clear, sharp, delineated.

I chose Life B.

In Life B, someone identified what was wrong inside me and had the tools necessary to fix it. I didn't think, then, of all of the things medicine cannot fix.

When you can't see the blackboard in your classroom, you know that your eyes need help; you don't think the board itself is the problem. When you can't see the good in your life, you think your life is all wrong. Depression tells you there is no help to be had, no quarter for refuge, no hand to hold. Depression tells you resistance is futile. It is the ultimate siren, seducing victims from deep within our own brains, convincing us that to crash upon the rocks and die won't simply ease our pain but is the answer to the pain we cause everyone around us.

In 2016, a new psychiatrist took a more extensive family and social history than I'd ever given before and, after several months, shared his diagnosis with me: double depression. He explained the concept of cycling at very low moods. Some physicians believe that people who suffer from double depression are really suffering from a form of bipolar disorder in which depressive episodes are only rarely and irregularly interrupted with a kind of mania.

In my case, I wasn't experiencing mania, exactly: my manic episodes consisted of those precious days and weeks during which I felt normal. In truth, I'd never known an ordinary day.

It's been six years since my diagnosis and my medications have allowed me a more stable neural existence. The most important thing about being more stable neurologically is that it makes me more stable mentally—and that means I take my medication consistently.

I am not going to get better. As my psychiatrist explained, I've had so many major depressive episodes that my brain, without medication, triggers those episodes on its own. In the same way that someone uses insulin to control diabetes or blood thinners to control dangerous clots, the medication helps prevent these episodes from occurring.

For years I believed that I could surmount my depression, overcome it, wrestle it into submission so that I could be normal. The diagnosis has allowed me to accept that normal may just mean being able to engage with my loved ones and my work. Normal means knowing I have a chronic illness and treating it so that I can do the things that make me feel content. It means accepting that life is good, no superlatives needed.

And that is the story of this book. My story is about making a decision about my well-being, about understanding that it was my choice. Not someone else's. Only mine. It sounds so simple, and sometimes, for some people, it is. For me, it wasn't. I had to break through many sets of expectations in order to understand that only I had the power to save my own life, and only I had the power to change it.

Life B

1

THE PROGENITORS

WHEN I WAS YOUNG, I DIDN'T KNOW I HAD A MENTAL illness. I didn't know what *mental illness* meant. But I did have two examples of mentally ill women in my life: my grandmothers.

––––

A memory from childhood: "Go take this upstairs to Grandma Sofie," says my mother, handing me a plate of the same dinner she's making for our family of four: pork chops, mashed potatoes, boiled carrots. I'm seven or eight, and I don't want to go up the short flight of stairs to my grandmother's room.

But I am an obedient child. I take the plate. We don't have anything as fancy as a tray. As I climb the wooden steps, regular family smells (cooking, dish soap, cut grass on the breeze through the living room windows) mix on the tiny landing with sun-warmed beaverboard and mildew from my grandmother's towels in the half bathroom. My grandmother lives in a small bedroom across from another small bedroom.

Grandma calls out, "Come in, dolly. I don't feel so good. Can you bring my supper to me?"

Usually she comes to the door, cracks it open a couple of inches,

3

and grabs the plate or bowl from my hands. This time I turn the doorknob and enter. Grandma Sofie, her iron-gray bob mussed from sleep, is lying on a bed pushed up against the far wall.

Grandma's room is strewn with knickknacks, china ornaments and costume jewelry, piles of magazines and paperbacks, bags of used clothing and table linens. On and between these she leaves the stuff of her daily life: empty ice cream containers and boxes of chocolates, tumblers of water and milk.

My grandmother lives on the second floor of our Cape Cod–style house because there is nowhere else for her to go. She grew up one of nine brothers and sisters in a Polish immigrant family. Her father Simon and mother Ann left the countryside near Krakow in 1912, landing in Newburgh, New York, on the Hudson River, because other Polish immigrants said it was a growing, prosperous city.

Family lore gleaned from aunts and uncles indicates that Sofie was "never right," although given the problems those aunts and uncles had, maybe no one in the family was "right." In 1932, Sofie married Jan Wojcik, a bricklayer, and their children Ann, Barbara (my mother), and Simon were born and raised in a neighborhood near the riverside filled with other Eastern European immigrants.

The Wojcik family moved frequently, due to financial troubles, Jan's alcoholism, and Sofie's conflicts with neighbors; she was prone to fights and name-calling. Jan spent very little time with anyone in the family from the 1950s until his death from alcoholism in the late 1960s. After a couple of stints as a psychiatric inpatient (and perhaps some electroconvulsive therapy, or ECT), Sofie found herself homeless, her siblings unwilling or unable to give her a place to stay, her oldest daughter Ann and her youngest son Marty living in crowded apartments. Only my mother Barbara, the middle child, had a room to spare.

I didn't have many friends as a child, partly because I wasn't allowed to have them visit even for outside games. My grandmother didn't like loud noises, and if we startled her by yelling during a round of tag or hopscotch, she might shout at us from the upstairs bathroom window.

While other friends scheduled sleepovers and suppers and marathon television-rerun-watching sessions, my younger sister and I waited to be invited to someone else's house—or kept our own company. Grandma was always around. She didn't like noise from children, but she made it herself, banging and crashing around at inconvenient hours of the day and night when she decided to sort some of her collections or cook something on her single hot plate. My sister and I were never allowed to invite anyone inside, except for the girls next door, whose parents already knew about our grandmother.

I must never talk about my grandmother, my mother told me. No one needs to know she lives with us if they don't have to, no one needs to know she is "crazy." If my teachers ask, our family includes a mother, a father, and two children.

My grandmother got to do whatever she liked. She didn't really exist.

Except that she did. She generated smells and trash and stories. Sometimes, when she had luck at the thrift stores she frequented, she brought back piles of comic books, vintage magazines, and yellowing paperbacks for me and my sister. *Richie Rich. Little Lulu. Katy Keene.* Edgar Cayce tales. We were greedy for this material, or at least I was. I couldn't get enough of the *Archie* comics that arrived in bundles tied with string, or the ghost stories, the kind they sold at the grocery store cash register that our mother didn't even glance at while waiting to check out and then head home to make dinner. I flipped through the magazines, gaping at glossy pages from the

1930s and '40s with their glamorous ads for camiknickers and mangle machines, imagining a different life.

For some reason my mother allowed of this kind of clutter. My sister Ellen and I were allowed to read, scribble, and color in the magazines, cut them up and use them for collage art. Maybe because it kept us reading. Maybe because it kept us quiet. Maybe because my mother was experiencing a rare moment of gratitude toward her mother.

When she moved downstairs into a basement area that my parents renovated at great effort and expense, where she had her own refrigerator and stove and oven, my grandmother's frequent meals gave off such a powerful aroma of onions that often my mother opened the door to the basement and yelled at her.

Grandma Sofie, to me, was like a child who got to do whatever she wanted. Most mornings, she put on a housedress, cardigan, and Keds. Usually she had an umbrella, in case of rain or to wave unsteadily at people who bothered her.

Everyone bothered Grandma. My sister and I didn't often see her on her daily route through the streets of Newburgh; we were safely ensconced in elementary school. Sometimes, when we came home, my mother would tell us we had to go next door so that she could drive downtown and pick up Grandma Sofie, who had gotten into an altercation and was too upset to take the bus.

Just before I left for college, subsidized housing for senior citizens opened up in a high-rise a few miles away from our house. My parents, weary of dealing with my grandmother's increased hoarding and filth, gratefully moved her to this safe place. Her apartment had a living room, a dining area, a galley kitchen, and a bedroom. For the next few years, until I got married and moved overseas, our house was home to just four people again, and no one had to talk about the madwoman in the cellar.

———

My maternal grandmother is my earliest memory of a person with mental illness, probably lifelong, that kept her on the margins of society. She couldn't work, live in close community with neighbors, or support herself.

But by "the margins of society," what I really mean is the margins of our family. Since we weren't allowed to talk about my grandmother, she didn't play a role in the rest of our lives with school, church, friends, or even other parts of my mother's family. I grew up believing that people with challenged brains should be kept separate.

At least if they were underserved and difficult, like Grandmother Sofie, who grew up with very little and lived with less after marrying Grandfather Jan and watching him descend into alcoholism. Along with her own mental challenges, Sofie Wojcik had very little money, no social status, and no job. But my other grandmother, my paternal grandmother, was also mentally ill—and yet we interacted with her regularly.

———

Grandmother Collier was born Emily Ann Wakefield to a privileged family in Massachusetts. Her childhood portraits show a happy and perhaps spoiled little girl, dark hair in ringlets, big blue eyes, starched tucks and ruffles on her white dresses, velvet trimming her winter coat and muff. She trained as a teacher and moved to Connecticut, where at some point she met my grandfather while he was studying for his master's degree at Yale University in New Haven. They must have married during the program because my father was born in that city. By the time my uncle was born two years later, the little family had relocated to New Jersey for my grandfather's job at the Edison Laboratory in Menlo Park.

Her severe postpartum depression after my uncle Matthew was born resulted in my grandmother's institutionalization, baby in tow. She may have undergone some kind of treatment that permanently changed her personality and behavior. While doing some slapdash genealogical research in the 1990s, I found my father's first cousin Lydia, who lives in Alabama, and spoke with her several times by telephone. The first time, she mentioned there was a family secret she couldn't share with me. The second time, she "accidentally" let slip that my grandmother Emily had had to be sent to the hospital with her infant son, a source of shame for all involved. "It was so sad, she had been such a sweet young wife."

My grandmother lived in the New Jersey house with my uncle from the time of her late-1940s divorce from my grandfather. We would drive from our house in New York to pick up my brothers Theodore (Theo) and Kenneth (Ken), children from my father's first marriage who lived an hour south. They were always waiting outside by their metal mailbox near the street and climbed into the backseat of our station wagon (my sister and I lying down or curled up in the way back); then we would head north again to see Grandma and Uncle Matthew.

Their house was nothing special: gray stucco with a front porch and a garage (so old-fashioned that its arched entrance consisted of two wooden doors that closed with a hasp). But it included that porch and garage, plus a dining room and a separate powder room, things our tiny house didn't. The rooms also contained good furniture, sturdy and attractive. My grandmother's house offered a promise that someone in my family once believed things would be better. That it was normal to have pretty things.

We always had something to eat at Grandmother's, which often seemed odd because my family ate an early lunch before leaving on our three-hour drive. I didn't understand that my adolescent brothers were always hungry or that setting out food and drink gave

Uncle Matthew and my mother something to do while the rest of us "visited." They would lay out sandwiches, cold cuts, cheese, a relish tray, Pepperidge Farm cookies, pitchers of milk and iced tea.

If it was fine weather, we might tumble around the small back-yard with its toolshed and vegetable garden. Uncle Matthew was very proud of his rhubarb. Sometimes he served it stewed, sweetened, and topped with cream or custard. I liked it, and I also liked being outside with two men and two boys, a huge change from the female-skewed dynamic at home. When we were outside, everyone relaxed. My father sprawled on the grass and watched my sister run in figure eights while my brothers tinkered with toy rockets or cars, whatever my parents or uncle bought as a sop for their lopsided existence.

But not every Sunday had fine weather, and sometimes we all had to crowd into the living room and talk. My uncle might disappear into his clock-fixing workshop in the cellar, my father to the garage under the pretext of tuning up their car, my brothers upstairs to read schoolbooks in a bedroom, but my sister and I were too little to do anything but sit on the sofa beneath my mother's watchful eyes—and our grandmother's blank ones.

Mostly Grandmother Collier sat in an armchair and worried. Did we have enough to eat? Is it going to rain? Has Benjamin finished with the automobile? My mother hated the useless chatter. If she couldn't be moving around with purpose, she'd at least liked to have had a nap before getting back in the car.

I took to reading the piles of *Yankee* magazines kept in baskets beside the sofa. By the time I was ten I was an expert on all things New England, scouring our cellar for items that might wind up in the *Yankee* "What the Hell Is It?" column. I studied the genealogical inquiries, hoping someone might ask a question about the Halls or Wakefields of my own family, wondering what people did when an actual connection was made.

My paternal grandmother unwittingly offered me a different view of how a person with mental illness exists. Because she'd received some professional education, because she met and married a man with more professional education, her daily life looked much different than Grandma Wojcik's. Grandma Collier lived in a nice house with her bachelor son, who not only cared for her but enjoyed her company. Her other son, my father, brought his blended family to visit her regularly, sometimes for extra visits over holidays like Christmas and Easter. She had clean clothes, a clean kitchen, money to buy us lovely gifts like hardcover books, boxes of candy, and fancy sweaters.

But I could see that she was also no more right than Grandma Wojcik. She didn't react much to anything, whether funny or charming or downright annoying. Her mind seemed to turn in circles that only allowed a little bit of the world in at a time. My sister and I knew Grandma Collier liked us. Maybe even loved us. But she wasn't sure how to talk to us, or to our older brothers.

Here, then, was a mentally ill woman who was not kept behind a closed door or shut off from family and community. I knew our grandmothers were not like other people's grandmothers. I remember asking my mother why we didn't have grandmothers who cooked and baked and talked with their grandchildren. Maybe fewer people have those kinds of grandmothers. I understood my two grandmothers were not just different. They were damaged. Is that what it meant to be mentally ill? That you were damaged?

My mother and father treated their own mothers, those unfit adults, with different levels of care and deference but a similar resignation. Neither Sofie Wojcik nor Emily Collier was treated as a respected elder with wisdom and experience worth imparting.

Neither of my grandmothers had a spouse with wisdom or experience worth imparting either. Grandmother Sofie had married Jan Wojcik, but for all my sister and I knew he was fictional, a ghost no one wanted to talk about or remember. I never met him, and I've never seen a picture of him either. Grandmother Emily was divorced at some point in the late 1940s. I did meet Henry Collier frequently as a small child, but then he and his second wife Delia moved to Perth, Australia, their presence in our lives confined to floppy blue airmail letters.

Both my grandfathers had their own mental health issues. Grandfather Jan, as I've mentioned, was an alcoholic whose substance addiction often resulted in violence against his family—and perhaps others. Grandfather Allan, who lost both parents within six months of each other when he was just twenty-one, was probably a genius (one of his patents funded that Australian retirement), with all the personality challenges that can imply. He was also a lifelong racist whose extreme hatred I saw up close when I visited Perth at age eighteen and heard him call people of color various despicable names.

But I saw so little of those men that they scarcely registered in my mind. They seemed unconnected to me—not even disconnected, because I didn't feel anything for either one of them in the first place. I did feel things for my grandmothers.

Both seemed untethered to real life, the daily existence that my family lived in: meals, school, work, play. Both my grandmothers made me anxious. Both seemed impossible to love or view with affection. Both my grandmothers were women who hadn't succeeded, which is what my parents wanted most for me and my sister.

Both my grandmothers were mentally ill.

What would it mean for my future, my chances of success, if I were also mentally ill? As I grew older and felt more and more like a misfit, in a state of constant sadness, I worried about how I might overcome this family misfortune. What would make me acceptable, able to take my place in the world?

———

Whether the madwoman is in the attic, the cellar, or the living room, she's rarely welcome at the table. I'm loosely using the phrase *madwoman in the attic*, which was made famous by Sandra Gilbert and Susan Gubar in their 1979 book of literary criticism that posited nineteenth-century women writers often located a madwoman, like *Jane Eyre*'s Mrs. Rochester, in an attic or another separate place, not just to keep her away from people considered more normal but because a madwoman's unleashed feelings frightened readers and writers.

Both my grandmothers frightened me when I was a child through their behavior, but now, as an adult, it is their fates that frighten me more. Now I know a little about what can happen to women unable to assume prescribed roles in society. About how failure happens, and how frightening it can be to watch other people succeed in making a living while you depend on other people but cannot follow their rules.

My grandmothers were born into a country with few options for women other than marriage and childbearing. They both married and bore children, but when their brains broke, they found themselves without support. Grandfather Wojcik vanished into addiction. Grandfather Collier slid from divorce into a second marriage and moved to a different continent.

My grandmothers' stories are relevant to how I learned about mental illness and how I thought about myself as I grew older and realized how severe my depression was. How would I make it through college? How would I support myself once I graduated? What would life as a depressed adult woman look like?

I asked myself those questions. Perhaps the key thing about any madwoman, in any room of the house, is that I wasn't asking them during rational moments. I was asking them in my worst, lowest moments, when all I wanted was to curl into the corner of my bed-room and cry about how lost I felt.

Meanwhile, across the room from me was my only sibling, my sister Ellen, who was fighting her own battle. Her experience was as different from mine as both our grandmothers' lives were from each other.

2

SNAKE HILL

MY MOTHER TELEPHONES, SOMETHING SHE RARELY does. "Email is my preferred method of communication," she often says, because unlike telephone calls to Virginia, email messages are free. But one day in 2013, she picks up the phone.

"Bethanne?" Her voice is strained, higher on the second syllable. She usually addresses me as Beth.

I clutch my phone a little more tightly, worried that she's going to tell me she's ill. I live seven hours away by car, but that's easier and probably quicker than trying to reach her Hudson Valley home through a combination of Amtrak, Metro-North train, and taxicab, or a bus from Port Authority. I start mental calculations; could I get there by the end of the day?

"I received a call from your cousin this morning," she says. "It was very upsetting. She told me her son is dead. She says a bunch of men attacked him and David up on Snake Hill."

My brain flips quickly through this story's blank spaces, creating a flowchart of connections. Janet is my first cousin, Aunt Ann's oldest of four; David is the youngest. Janet is in her late fifties, David in his late forties. Jackson is, or was, about twenty-five, a child Janet had with an unknown man. I have never met Jackson.

I haven't seen or spoken with Janet in decades. I haven't seen or spoken with David for the same amount of time.

These are strangers.

These are strangers, right?

My mother is shaken. "I don't want to get involved in their mess," she keeps saying. "I don't want to be involved in this."

Who is asking her to be involved? What does she mean by mess? As I often have to do with my mother when she's particularly rattled, I pick things apart slowly and ask a lot of questions, over and over again. When did this happen? Where is Janet? Is David dead, alive, hurt? Who discovered that Jackson was dead? What men did this? Why were Jackson and his uncle up on Snake Hill to begin with?

The conversation is slow and halting. A great deal remains unsaid, because my mother does not like to poke around places that are tender at the bone, marrow-deep memories of stored pain. I finally figure out that David involved his teenage nephew in drug deals. The otherwise undescribed men were probably members of a violent gang that middle-aged David had cheated. Maybe they surprised David and Jackson at the pond on Snake Hill; maybe it's a place they often take traitors and con men.

David "cut his leg badly" and ran away. Was Jackson already dead? Or did David leave his nephew alone?

I get off the phone and start to cry.

A year or so later I'm again on a telephone call, this time with a friend who always has a crazy story to share. She's telling me about her father, a man with an outsized personality that matched the tall tales he told and the love my friend had for him. After she relates a near crime he committed that involved a lake, a pickup truck, and an undocumented immigrant, I wipe tears of laughter from my eyes and say, "God, that reminds me of the story about my cousins . . ." I give her my packaged version of Jackson's death (murder?).

She laughs but then says, "You know, I don't think you should tell people stories about your family." She's heard quite a few of them. "They're really messed up."

I hear, *You're messed up. You're too much. This is unsavory.*

I could hear, *How tragic. What is the real story?*

––––

Epigenetics explains, in part, that we carry the memories of our ancestors within us. What a concept—to be not just the tellers of stories, the listeners to stories, but the bearers of stories, in our bones.

Some people know a great deal about their family: history, genealogy, tall tales. Some know almost nothing. I'm somewhere in the middle. I know a lot of anecdotes. But it's all mostly hearsay. That's because, in an effort to protect me and my sister, my mother kept us separate from most of her relatives and some of my father's. We weren't supposed to accept the darkness and vitriol and despair from those people, although as a child I just assumed we weren't supposed to wear polyester or argue at picnics or settle for blue-collar jobs.

I once thought I could tell these stories blithely, as I did to my friend on the phone. I was wrong. My pain from carrying these stories in my body had to be obliterated by tossing them off as if they didn't matter, as if they were entertainment instead of things that happened to human beings.

Versions of sad and even tragic family episodes became literary macarons for me. Light, delicious, and easy to consume. I had short and long versions, depending on the occasion, my mood, and the identity of the listener. I could elicit gasps or guffaws. It helps us keep pain at arm's length.

It helped me keep pain not just away but contained.

One of my time-tested arm's-length techniques is to refer to my city of origin as "my benighted hometown." Newburgh, New

York, once referred to as the Queen of the Hudson, named in the 1960s an All-American Town, is now a sad place. North of Manhattan, south of Poughkeepsie, on the opposite side of the Hudson River from both, it is, statistically, the murder capital of New York State. When I was in high school, one week *The New York Times Sunday Magazine* ran a bright-yellow cover under the headline "Will the Last Person Leaving Newburgh Please Turn Out the Lights?" And that was when the biggest problems were coke dens on Broadway and homemade bombs in high school race riots.

Newburgh in the twenty-first century is a place I've never called home. I left in the 1980s and rarely visit.

What I know—and anyone could, just as easily—comes from news reports and my mother's dispatches. The MS-13 has its headquarters in Poughkeepsie, the Latin Kings in Newburgh. "Despite its small size and bucolic setting, Newburgh occupies one of the most dangerous four-mile stretches in the northeastern United States," reported *New York Magazine* in 2011.

About a mile south of Newburgh is the suburb of New Windsor, where I was raised. Like Newburgh, New Windsor hugs the spectacularly beautiful Hudson River and its highlands. Every day when my elementary school bus hit the crest of the hill down to my neighborhood, I could see the river and the mountains across it—a view imprinted in my consciousness as surely as any family memory.

At about that same elevation a quarter mile north is Snake Hill. Its panoramic views are stunning. You can see for miles as you stand on bones of the marginalized dead, fossils of legless reptiles, and memories that no one else shares.

There's also a pond where my cousin's son drowned. Where my own cousin drowned.

Jackson's loss cannot be one of the stories I carry in my bones, in my DNA. He was not my predecessor, my ancestor. He was supposed to be a new generation—progeny, the future—like my own daughters, his cousins, who don't know his name, who don't even know he existed.

In the past decade or so, I've read a lot about the importance of a family narrative for children. Sharing the things that make your family special and bind you together makes young people feel stronger and may even make them healthier. My daughters say, whenever they learn some new fact about their heritage, "Why didn't anyone ever tell me this before?" They are outraged that any knowledge would be kept from them.

Now that they are both adults, I've shared some of the harder facts from the family narrative they feel they've missed. When I tell them something difficult, they cry, "Why are you telling me this?" Maybe I don't need to tell them. Maybe it's already in their bones.

But they don't know Jackson's story, whether it's in their bones or not.

———

When I was thirteen, my cousin Janet killed her husband Greg. She was only eighteen, but that was old enough to stand trial as an adult and be sentenced to twenty years in prison.

Janet and Greg married young. There were in love, poor, working-class, and why not? They lived in a trailer out in the woods. Shotguns hung on the wall because they hunted game for food. Janet suffered from terrible scoliosis but was too scared to undergo surgery, even though my mother offered to foot the bill. Instead, Janet took tranquilizers to deal with the pain. One night those pills made her hallucinate that her husband, coming home from work, was the devil. She knew how to use a rifle. She did.

Jackson was born years after Janet served her sentence, commuted for good behavior. For a while, all I knew of her was that my mother said she found God, had a baby, and was trying hard to hang on to a job in the town farther upstate where she'd settled.

I don't know her story. It might be in my bones, but I've never been given any details. And my mother prefers not to tell it. "I don't want to be involved in that mess," she says whenever the topic of Cousin Janet comes up, which is infrequently.

I have no idea why my mother didn't want to be involved, why and when she pulled away from her sister and nieces and nephews, and I have even less of an idea about how she kept me and my sister far removed from the "mess." I don't know how to talk with my mother about this terrible, sad thing that happened.

Whose memories are in your bones and mine that have brought us to this impasse?

SNAKE HILL IS less than half a mile's walk from the house where I grew up. That's the house where my mother lived until 2021, its fifteen-thousand-dollar mortgage long since paid off, the trees in our backyard the same varieties that grow on the Hill.

The whole time I was growing up, my sister and I were warned that you didn't go to Snake Hill. It was dangerous, too dangerous to hike as children. Too dangerous to hike if you're a young woman.

What was up there, in that dark place? This was forty years before Jackson's death.

Dark places litter my mother's family tree like trash blown by wind against branches and power lines. Here and there, alcoholism; a short distance away, drug addiction and sexual promiscuity; on that high place, schizophrenia and bipolar syndrome.

My depression is just one leaf on a twig, really. But a leaf on a twig contains the same genetic material as the rest of the tree. Take a cutting and you can grow a sapling. A sapling won't progress into a mature oak or elm or maple if it isn't safe, if it doesn't receive the sun, air, and water that allow it to send out roots. My mother wanted her children to grow into the kind of stable trees she loved and cared for in her small patch of suburbia. She was trying to protect us from all the ways children can be cut down. The way my cousin Jackson was cut down.

But as I've discovered through a life of struggling with mental illness, prune as you will, some plants contain seeds of their own destruction. I recently learned that a certain kind of cedar tree native to Virginia no longer exists. The oldest trees are still there, and they send out seeds that grow into weak two- and three-foot-high leafy things—but at some point, some kind of insect infected the cedars at a cellular level so that they kill themselves automatically. There's nothing anyone can do, at least right now, to change that cycle.

———

Cousin Janet has three siblings. The oldest is Walt, who rarely plays with the rest of us; by the time I am old enough to notice my first cousins, he's already a sulky adolescent, although he isn't unkind. Janet's slightly younger sister Sally is my idol, with her cute nose and curly hair. The youngest is David, who is a little too rambunctious most of the time, according to my mother.

Ann's husband, my uncle Ken Bradley, doesn't participate in many social occasions. He is an amiable, wide-faced man who runs an odd, crowded little appliance repair shop downtown where my mother sometimes brings us when she needs to drop off a loan for her sister. I can't remember how old I am when my mother tells me that Ken is an alcoholic. Not the kind who hits anyone (like her father) but the kind who just drinks all the time. "He probably drinks beer while he works," she says, her voice ripe with disapproval. She loves her sister deeply but cannot offer any compassion toward a person who would allow liquor to jeopardize a paycheck.

The Bradley kids are an endless source of worry for my mother. Once Walt, threatening to drop out of high school, is sent to stay with us for a couple of weeks. Does it make any difference? Who knows? A few years later when Janet shoots Greg, my mother will be sure to write to her in prison, to send her packages of allowed items. For many, many years my mother will help her niece Sally and nephew David with their lives and their finances.

Aunt Ann and her family live in a place known to me only as the Bradshaw Apartments, a sad-looking complex just a couple of miles from our suburban home. My mother will say while we're out shopping, "I have to stop at the Bradshaw Apartments," meaning I have to bring some groceries or drugstore staples to my sister, because she doesn't have what we have. At the Bradshaw apartment, the rooms smell of the cigarettes Aunt Ann and Uncle Walt chain-smoke; the walls are coated with nicotine. Can it possibly be right, in my memory, that those walls had nothing on them? No art, no photographs, nothing? I think it is right. Ann and Walt had enough to worry about without fussing over that.

When we're there, we rarely sit in the living room with its green Naugahyde sofa. We run around in the building's little courtyard with its sparse grass and little defining fence, play with Aunt Ann's cats, or go upstairs to the girls' room and allow our blond, frizzy-haired cousins to braid our fine, silky tresses. We're never there for very long anyway. These are not social visits over coffee and cake. My mother might accept an iced tea or a couple of packaged cookies, but before an hour is up she's bustling us back to our station wagon with some sort of farewell like, "We have to get to the store before Ben comes home," or "Bethanne has an appointment with the allergy doctor."

Sometimes I, with my many allergies, including tobacco smoke and cats, wonder why my mother brings me along on these visits when they make me wheeze and cough. Somehow I know I am never, ever to ask that question, that going to see the Bradleys is a duty so sacrosanct that it supersedes my health. People who don't have as much as we do matter more than anything else.

You are not supposed to have more than anyone else. You are not supposed to be safe and fed and clothed. These are the messages my mother's face and body and words communicate to me when we make a stop at the Bradshaw Apartments. Now I understand that she was ashamed, ashamed to be in a place in life so much better than her older sister's. It must have been painful to walk in and even more painful to walk out.

Many years in the future, Aunt Ann has become a prison guard, moved to a different place where Sally and her children can live, and is ill with some sort of cancer that has caused most of one ear to be removed. I am about to get married and my mother has decreed that none of her relatives will be invited, to save me from "that mess."

My mother tells me my aunt would like to see me, that she knows she isn't invited to my wedding but would like to give me a gift before I move to Germany. I say of course; although I do not feel connected to her family, I do love Aunt Ann, who has always treated me like a person and not a child.

When we arrive, Aunt Ann fusses over serving tea and cookies, wanting to do the right thing. Like me she is vain, and I can tell from the constant fidgeting with her hair on that side of her head that she worries about whether her altered ear is covered. I've brought a large coffee-table book of Maurice Sendak art because my aunt and my mother and I share a passion for his work. We sit on a tiny back porch in the late-autumn sun and page through the volume. It's a good visit.

Months later during a telephone call, my mother tells me, "My sister was so happy to see you last fall. She told me, 'You've raised such a kind and generous daughter.'"

My new husband and I are still living overseas when Aunt Ann moves in with my parents. The cancer has worsened. My mother outfits a spare room with a hospital bed and nurses her sister through death.

Ann Bradley's will designates my mother as executrix and has a special fund for Ann's grandchildren so that none of them, no matter when they are born and no matter how old they grow, will ever go without shoes.

Every time I think of that—a fund so that her grandchildren will never go barefoot—my stomach crumples and my eyes tear up. In my circles, people talk about legacies and retirement funds and heirlooms. My aunt, a humble woman who made mistakes but never shirked hard work, did not want her grandchildren to go without something so basic.

My mother took Cousin Sally's children, four children from three different fathers, on annual shopping trips to buy those shoes. Ann did not want her own children to have access to the money; she was afraid they would squander it on drugs and booze and nightlife. She never dreamed that her son David would involve his nephew in drug deals. Now there is one less grandchild who needs shoes.

In their bones, all Aunt Ann's children carried the snakes of addiction. Did they come from her father? From their father? Does it matter?

———

There aren't any links to an obituary for Jackson Bradley or to a crime log for David Bradley. I've looked and looked. If I wanted to find out more, I am sure I could search through library reference books and newspapers online. I could drive to New York State and look through archives in the Newburgh city library. I could try to discover secrets, to uncover texts and photos and recordings and sketches in pursuit of my family's truth.

I don't have any of that when it comes to my family. Yes, my mother keeps a file of history, but it's full of celebrations: my grandmother in an elaborate First Communion dress, weddings, baptisms, the occasional graduation. There are no photos of people inebriated, or articles about incarcerations, or diaries about abuse. There's a half-hearted family tree and a few official certificates.

Even when it comes to family records, history belongs to the winners. Or the purported winners. Sometimes a little girl in a fancy white Communion dress grows up to be a sad, abandoned wife. Or a desperately ill alcoholic.

My mother is, rightly, terrified of alcohol and drugs. She has married out of her class and milieu and even though she isn't high up the ladder she's going to make sure she doesn't slip so much as a rung. When researchers discover that addiction often skips a generation from grandparents to grandchildren, she starts watching my sister and me like a hawk, worrying about every glass of wine she sees me drink in public and every cigarette my sister smokes in secret.

She doesn't know enough, no one knows enough, to be terrified of what's behind too many glasses of wine, too many packs of cigarettes, or—let's be honest about my poor cousins here—too much meth. She doesn't understand that the mess she's afraid of exists in her bones, and in ours.

————

Sometimes Cousin Janet pings me on Facebook Messenger. "Hi Cousin!" she will write. "How are You? How is your sister? Your

Mom?" Her typing has its own rules, and so does her spelling, as I discover the few times I answer her.

A good story would have me answering Janet at length, then setting up a weekend to meet and have a reunion. Maybe one day, at my mother's funeral, I will see Janet and one or more of her siblings, and we will hug.

But a good story with a happy ending isn't possible without good narrative structure, a family narrative that includes bonds between cousins, the kind that don't shed their skins over the years when truly bad things happen. My mother wasn't trying to reject her niece Janet, or any of her other relatives. She did choose to put her own children first and, in doing so, hoped she had saved us from some of life's dangers.

3

—

BITTER ROOTS

I NOTICED MY YOUNGER SISTER'S CHALLENGES LONG before there was any kind of medical language attached to them. I didn't see my own, although I felt them. I suspect it was somewhat similar for her.

My parents were big John Denver fans, with his greatest hits in heavy rotation. Each time "Grandma's Feather Bed" came on, Ellen would spin into a barefoot version of a clog dance. Grown-up visitors loved it. "So cute!" they would say as my six-year-old sister began to hop and wave.

Now in her fifties, during one bout of mania in 2017, Ellen stayed up many nights until the wee hours, smoking, drinking, and dancing, dancing, dancing—movement becomes essential to her during manic phases, which often start in February and end sometime in early fall, when she can crash into a debilitating depression.

A few years ago, before she began a series of ECT treatments meant to calm her rapid cycling between mania and depression, she progressed from singing along to a tape to trying to put together a band with several of the other karaoke-bar regulars; I knew this from her sporadic Facebook updates.

Mental illnesses rarely follow a recognizable path. One of the reasons for this is the trouble with understanding the diagnoses and how those diagnoses should be treated. We often still say "mental illness" rather than simply "illness" because illnesses of the brain—depression, schizophrenia, bipolar syndrome—so often go hand in hand with personality disorders—narcissism, borderline, sociopathy. Because they are not physical in nature, they require a completely different course of treatment. Personality disorders don't respond to pharmaceuticals. They can be greatly aided by therapy, but the person with the disorder must be willing to engage in that therapy in order to be helped.

In the decades since my sister's childhood dancing, I've read a lot about mental illness and personality disorders. I've learned that you can have one without the other; for example, I know quite a few people who are bipolar but do not have personality disorders and are able to maintain high-functioning and healthy lives as long as they take their medication. I've learned that bipolar disorder has a strong inherited component and runs through families just like jawlines and toe length. My mother has also learned a lot and has attended National Alliance on Mental Illness (NAMI) meetings and workshops. She conducts internet research and reads books about manic depression and how to help children with bipolar parents with my sister's now-adolescent son in mind.

When we were young, I didn't understand that my sister had bipolar disorder, and I didn't understand that she had borderline personality disorder, any more than I understood that I had double depression. What I knew was that she always wanted to be closer to me. Sitting closer. Playing closer. Doing whatever it was I was doing. Even at a young age I was uncomfortable with that degree of closeness, but it took me until middle age to articulate why to my therapist.

"It bothered me. It made me uncomfortable," I told her.

"What feeling is behind being uncomfortable?"

I fidgeted. I didn't know. I breathed deeply a few times. "She didn't just want to be close to me. She wanted to be part of me. She would have crawled right into me if she could have."

An upward glance from Ms. Therapist. "What would be wrong with that, with her crawling right into you?"

"It would mean that I am not an individual, that I am not myself."

"And if you are not yourself?"

"Then I'm nothing."

———

The year 2007. We pulled up in the driveway of our family house on Cape Cod and there my sister sat, in a wicker porch chair, a cigarette in one hand and a longneck in the other. Once upon a time she would have been holding an iced tea, maybe a dog on a leash, but things had changed.

She wasn't supposed to be there. Adam and I had planned a family vacation to the Cape for us and our two children, but Ellen had driven all the way up from her own northern Virginia home on the assumption that we would welcome her presence. It didn't matter to our daughters, a tween and a teen, who spilled out of the car and ran over to their aunt Ellen before I'd even unfastened my seatbelt.

Ellen got up and started to dance to the Miley Cyrus song playing on her iPod. The girls laughed and joined in, singing about a party in the USA. They were happy to see her.

All I could see were the cigarette and the bottle and the wild look in her eyes. My mother appeared from around the side of the house, holding an armful of weeds she'd spent the cooler morning hours pulling from the garden beds. My mother wasn't supposed to be there either, but as she told me later, she'd chosen to come along because she was nervous about how Ellen might behave.

My husband and I bought the house on Cape Cod with my parents in 1999. The rationale was that Ellen and her then husband, who at the time lived in Massachusetts, would be able to enjoy time there with my parents during the year, while Adam and I could visit on holidays and during the summer.

Things went wrong from the start. My parents were ambivalent about having a second home and joining a community to which they had few ties. A few years after we purchased the house, Ellen's husband accepted a job offer in Washington, D.C., and their family left Massachusetts, rarely able to spend their own, separate time on Cape Cod. I wanted to spend time there with my nuclear family alone, while Ellen longed for more time with us. Even though the house had room for everyone, it didn't fit our families very well.

Ellen swept our daughters inside with promises of soda and candy and a trip to the kettle pond for dog walking and swimming. Fun! Aunt Ellen is Always! Fun! I could already see she was in a manic phase, even though it would take me several more years to understand when those cycles started and ended. During summers, she was almost always ebulliently happy, but during those years I saw less of her in the seasons when she was barely able to leave her bed for weeks at a time, eating so little that she was nearly gaunt at our father's 2007 memorial service. At that time, my mother confessed to me that she'd been buying cases of Ensure to try and coax Ellen into eating something, anything.

Now, on the Cape, just months later, she was up for anything, nothing could bother her, not even my grumpy scolding "They haven't had lunch yet" able to bring her down to earth.

I wouldn't know for another decade that my grumpiness and fatigue have the same source as her elation and energy. We were both cycling, but I don't experience mania. Part of my deep-seated antipathy toward my sister was her strangeness to me, her otherness. I never felt the highs she felt. If empathy requires being able to share in the emotional state of the person you're with, I had no empathy toward her.

I never have.

_____

My sister and I share the same roots. We share more of the same DNA than any other two people in the world.

But those roots are more bitter to me than sweet. I cannot see a "Birth made us sisters, life made us friends" greeting card without frowning. The older I get, the more I interact with my sister, the less time I want to spend with her. When we were children, she frightened me any chance she got. We'd play with the Ouija board, and she would make up characters that spewed epithets, characters I believed were real, because how would such a little kid know such terrible phrases? She would hit me, slap me, kick me, shove me into closets, and lock me out of the house. I became an object of her outbursts.

I saw other kids around me grow up with "normal" sibling relationships, but I felt tortured by my relationship with Ellen. It didn't feel normal. It didn't feel right. It didn't feel like the relationships between my friends and their siblings. It felt sad and shameful and lonely.

As we got older, I jumped at every chance to leave home and stay away from my family. Summer school for the arts. A trip overseas. A job near the ocean. College in a different state. Marriage, then a move to Europe. Anything to reclaim my boundaries, which shifted in a distinctly uncomfortable way every time I spent time with my sister.

But she did not stop wanting contact with me. She visited me in college and made my friends so anxious with her strange, negative stories about me that they told me point-blank they preferred not to spend time with her again. She visited me in the overseas apartment I shared with my new husband and spent most of the time sitting in the stairwell chain-smoking. She visited us while we were in grad school and poked fun at our house, our routine, and even the size of my bras on a drying rack.

My sister was always clamoring for more. More visits, more time, more information. "What is it you *do* each day?" she asked on more than one occasion. "I don't understand what you do! Why can't you explain to me how your morning goes? What do you have for breakfast? When do you sit down to work? Do you mostly write, or do you do other things too?"

I became more loath to share. She'd alienated so many of my friends that I didn't want to give her news of the old ones or access to the new ones. The more I told her about my schedule, the more she wanted to be included in it.

Who is my sister? What is she like? I wish I could tell you, but I've spent so much time holding her at arm's length, peering at her from between my fingers, that I don't think I really know. We come from the same roots but have grown apart.

To me, my sister was dangerous. She filled me with anxiety and dread. If I looked too closely at her, I would learn about parts of myself I didn't want to see.

When I was in my late thirties, I started building a career as a freelance writer. This involved occasional conferences. On one trip to a shabby-chic upstate New York inn, I met another writer who had recently published her first book, about something I'd never heard of before: borderline personality disorder.

As my colleague explained why she wrote the book—her mother was a borderline, as those in the know say—I felt uncomfortable pangs of recognition. She talked about inconsistencies:

tantrums and overreactions. She talked about feeling everything is your fault, about tiptoeing around a person because you never knew what they'd do next.

My mother isn't a borderline. She's often angry and frustrated, but she's clear about why, at least with me, and she is anything but inconsistent: Day after day, she made our lunches and ferried us to after-school activities and cleaned our clothes and soothed our hurts. She's stable and loyal and careful.

But her mother wasn't.

My mother grew up with a borderline parent who also suffered from mental illness. The two aren't necessarily connected; you can have either one without the other. But when they are connected—when a person with, say, schizoaffective disorder is also a narcissist—trouble is magnified.

My mother is well accustomed to living with a person who has mental illness and a personality disorder, a person who received no treatment for either. To her, caring for someone with these problems is the stuff of daily life. She allowed her mother, who was treated for both bipolar syndrome and psychotic episodes, to move in to a second-floor bedroom in our tiny family home. My mother may not like mental illness, but she is used to it and sees it as the way things are.

But I don't. Somehow, even with my grandmother living in our house and my sister growing up next to me, I only know that their way is not mine.

———

My husband and I decided to cut short our Cape vacation. We wanted to spend time together as a family, not with Ellen and her much-younger son and my mother, whose schedules didn't sync well with ours. "I don't think Ellen wants to go to the beach today." "He won't eat that for dinner." "Mom doesn't feel well."

We packed up the car, and I agreed to take the first shift driving back to Virginia. Adam was making a last sweep through the house for discarded sunglasses and sandals while the girls played on the porch with their cousin. I slid behind the wheel, and as I adjusted the mirrors, my sister hopped into the passenger seat.

My muscles instantly tensed. What does she want now?

"Beth, I want you to have a copy of this." She pointed at me with a paperback book. "It's all about borderline personality disorder. I have it. We all have it. You need to read this."

Her eyes were wild again, darting back and forth. "Thanks," I said, "but I'm not a borderline. But I'll read it if you want me to."

She wouldn't stop. She moved closer. "Yes, you are. You are, and Mom is, and we all need to learn more about this if we're ever going to get better, if we're ever going to be a family." She started to cry.

Ellen exhorted me to confess that I, too, was a borderline. I remained impassive, almost numb, to her dramatic behavior, trying to remember what my current therapist said, that I did not exhibit signs of a personality disorder and that I did not have to engage in circular arguments with my sister. When Adam came out with Emma and Martha, he said, "What's going on?" My sister got out and walked to the house, still crying.

I read the book when I got home. I read how those with a family history of the illness are five times more likely to have the condition. I also read how those diagnosed with it engage in risky or impulsive behavior and maintain unstable relationships. It was quite familiar to me due to my sister's behavior.

Borderline behavior is what I grew up with for eighteen years—my sister's and my grandmother's. Since my mother and father never discussed either one's behavior and certainly never identified my sister's behavior as anything but normal, I believed that the interactions I had with her were the interactions everyone had with their sisters. I didn't know that there might be different ways of relating to a sibling for quite a while.

I was taught that borderline behavior was normal. My parents weren't trying to teach that lesson. They were doing the best they could with what they had.

Ellen left the car but not my consciousness. It would be years before I understood something essential about Ellen wanting me to claim borderline status: if I did, we would be the same, at last.

———

My ambivalence about my sister has much to do with my own inability to put myself in her shoes. I'm afraid to, afraid that identifying with her will mean that I have to own all her upsetting behavior. I am trying too hard, have been trying for so long, to maintain some stability in my own life. I need to maintain boundaries around people whose behavior is unpredictable, from friends and coworkers to relatives.

In the decade since that trip to Cape Cod, a lot has changed. We sold the house. My mother built a sort of apartment onto my sister's Virginia home, where she stayed until selling that house and beginning to make arrangements for a move to a senior-living facility. Our daughters grew up and left home; our nephew is eighteen and lives in an apartment with my sister.

I have to accept what is my business and what is not. The last straw for me came on a vacation with my husband in 2015, when my ex-brother-in-law interrupted a romantic birthday dinner by calling, for what must have been the twentieth time that summer, and declaring he was ready to take their son and leave. I stood in an anteroom of our hotel trying to keep a signal and talk him down from his anxious state. I thought to myself, What am I doing? This is their drama. Not mine. I told my ex-brother-in-law that I was there anytime he needed me to stay with their son, but that right now I had to return to my meal.

Since that night, I've kept my distance from my sister, her ex-husband, and—unfortunately—their son. My distance is painful for my mother, who like any mother would like nothing better than to have her two children and their families connect.

But this distance has been necessary for me, a way for me to sift through the weeds in our shared history. The whirling dervish of a little girl is now a middle-aged woman. Sometimes—usually late in the year, during autumn's gray, sad days—Ellen turns from manic to depressive, writes awkward apologies, and spends her days and nights at home. The holidays pass, and she feels lonely. My mother spends much of her time with Ellen and her son.

Each spring, when the crocuses push through, so does my sister's next manic phase. Usually then I know I can find my mother kneeling in the garden beds, digging her spade in to find what she hopes will be healthy soil.

4

ROSIN ON THE BOW

L IVING WITH MY YOUNGER SISTER WAS DIFFICULT, but what made it especially so was that I truly didn't understand that the way our family worked wasn't the way all families worked. At the same time, I also felt something wasn't right about the way mine worked. My mother's imprecations not to talk about my grandmother extended to not talking about the way the rest of our small family communicated. I was not to talk about my father's unpredictable rages, my sister's unpredictable moods, or my own struggles with sadness.

When I was a young teenager and saw the *Saturday Night Live* skit "The Coneheads," I felt a shock of recognition. The Coneheads, a family from outer space with giant pointed heads, know that they're different from everyone else, but they are so different they think if they mimic the customs and manners of their new home no one will notice their difference. I knew immediately that our family was engaged in a similar sort of subterfuge.

By the time I reached adolescence, one thing I did know was that the subterfuge was supposedly for our benefit, mine and my sister's. If we didn't fall in line behind my mother's plans, we'd never get the highest grades, win the important prizes, and earn acceptances to the best colleges. That was the plan. That was her plan. We absorbed it all. I don't remember a time when I ever considered any path for myself other than attending a top-tier private college. It was what all the hard work was for. It was what the subterfuge was for.

————

We were born at the tail end of the baby boom, Ellen and I, too young to experience the 1960s and too old to crack the glass ceiling. There would be no counterculture for us, because only good girls who listened to their parents had any chance for success, and the one thing everyone in the America we were born into could agree on was that success involved progress and achievement. Many of our friends would receive one dollar for every A on their report cards or receive a long-yearned-for toy if they did well. We were expected to bring home perfect grades, and there was no celebration of them.

This tiger-mother attitude raised generations of children who may have chafed at maternal strictures but didn't find themselves with festering wounds from that chafing. For me, the combination of a genetic tendency toward depression combined with a familial expectation of excellence might as well have been regular beatings. The higher the standards my parents expected of me, the more chances there were for failure, and every failure set off the ticking clock of my internal critic's voice: *Not good enough. What a loser. You'll never make it. Why even try?*

I'm not sure how my mother conducted her near-professional anthropological study of the upper classes, but in the years between leaving home at eighteen and marrying my father at twenty-six, between her job at a small women's college, her WASPy dentist boss, and her forays to Manhattan, she'd gleaned that good grades were not enough. We would also need to play instruments, participate in sports, learn second languages, and earn more Girl Scout badges than actually fit on a sash.

————

I don't think I ever rosin my bow correctly. Dust, dust, dust, dust, all over my fingers and usually all over my violin, too, but is it getting into the horsehair, where it's supposed to be? I lack the patience to wait for the perfect friction between the dust and the hair, that moment when there's enough of one (rosin) to slide up the other (horsehair bow) and make it capable of vibrating the strings. I just want it to be ready. I don't want to wait.

Tighten the screw at the end of the bow. Not too much! That's too tight. Everything is supposed to be just right, just so, and I never want to bother. I never do. I just want to get to the music. Why can't someone else do all the preparation for me? Really, why can't someone else just hold the violin and bow for me so I can think the sounds and make them right? It's all too much, the tuning and positioning. How I am supposed to keep breathing and connect to the music?

Because once I get to the music, well, then it's all fine. If I am allowed to play, just play, it's fine. Of course, that rarely happens. You're supposed to practice, and practicing means you don't get to the melody, you don't get to slide into the rhythm and feel its sweet, pure shimmer. When you practice, you have to repeat notes, and not always in a pretty way. You have to correct notes, and that is tedious. Scratch, scratch, *zang*. Earsplitting chords. Unbearable shifts to high notes.

Without practice, that melody and rhythm don't exist. I know that. I know it, but I still don't want to practice, don't like to practice, don't want to split the music that I know is there into its quantum parts. Once I've heard it—through my teacher's playing, or on a record—I just want to hear it again. I want it to burst, fully formed, from the belly of my fiddle (the better the violin teacher, the more attached he or she will be to referring to the instrument as a fiddle).

Thus, it's devastating when it doesn't. My fingers can't find the right spots, don't slide where they should, and my bow arm has a mind of its own. Where is the tune I heard just minutes earlier? Why won't it flow from my playing the way it does from my teacher's? I know I want it to. Why isn't the wanting enough?

It will take me decades to understand that the wanting is never enough. Whatever you yearn for takes effort. If your first attempt is on point, you're either a prodigy or lucky, and your first attempt will not repeat itself. I learn that quickly, but it doesn't keep me from wishing it could.

Effort—practice, preparation, follow-through—these things are too much for me, and I'm not sure why. It isn't because I don't see their value. I watch my mother fill in her calendar and fill out her various volunteer forms; her handwriting is clear and precise, and she makes sure she has information correct. I watch my father plane a piece of wood for a bench and hear him remind me, "Measure twice, cut once," and he does. He always does. He never cuts corners, even when he's cutting a corner.

My parents aim for precision. Precise cuts and precise budgets make for a workable life.

I understand why my mother seeks precision; her childhood was filled with chaos. To my mother, the hiss of a steam iron is the sound of a home where family members own clothes worth dewrinkling. But I am less sure about my father's need for precision. I know he is an engineer, and engineers like things to work.

————

The violin was not my first choice. In my public school, in fourth grade you were allowed to take music lessons on the instrument of your choice, and mine was the clarinet. Failing that, the flute. Those were the instruments the cool kids chose, if any kids choosing to take music lessons could be deemed cool.

However, my mother worked for a dentist, and she knew that the embouchure required for wind instruments could cause bite problems, so no clarinet or flute for me. I was not-so-gently steered toward the violin, the music teacher's favorite—both she and her daughter played the violin. Mrs. Denny was cold and aloof, with icy blue eyes that seemed to catch every fingering and posture mistake, but you could tell she loved string instruments and she loved the music they played. I hated making mistakes, but I loved it when Mrs. Denny told me I'd gotten something right. That felt like my paternal grandmother's balsam-filled calico cat, sweet-smelling and just the right size.

My sister, two and a half years younger than me, was in first grade. She would have to wait three years before taking her own music lessons.

Except she didn't. Because 1972 was the height of Suzuki Method fever in the United States, and Mrs. Denny decided to start a group at our school with first and second graders. The Suzuki Method was pioneered by Japanese Dr. Shinichi Suzuki as a teaching philosophy in which fostering music as a sort of second language would also foster good moral character.

Given how much I loved my violin lessons and how fascinated my sister was with my violin itself, our mother wasted no time in signing Ellen up for the new school group. She proved to be a natural musician, and before long, not only were all of Mrs. Denny's students in every grade using Suzuki workbooks but my mother had begun dragging us to Suzuki workshops in our region; there was at least one summer Suzuki camp way upstate.

Before Suzuki, we played adaptations of classical tunes. After Suzuki, we played endless rounds of "Mississippi Hot Dog" and

"Go Tell Aunt Rhody," screeching repetitive rhythms that were designed to furrow grooves in our brains. I hated it. I hated Suzuki for its groupthink mentality. Nothing made Suzuki teachers and parents happier than an auditorium of fifty, one hundred, two hundred or more students all bowing in tandem to "Perpetual Motion" or "Allegretto." Even as a child I didn't want to be part of any club that would have me as a member.

I also hated what happened to my mother (and, eventually, father) in the Suzuki universe. She was the person who introduced me to the idea of defying authority. Her favorite music was folk. She not only listened to Joan Baez and Odetta and Miriam Makeba and the Weavers, but she also believed in the politics of Baez and Seeger and their comrades. She taught me to care about individuals, to be wary of mobs and mind control. Yet here she was, packing the car with a cooler of snacks, a tote bag of music, making sure our violins had their little snakelike foam humidifiers inserted so that we could drive to another Suzuki gathering. She'd drunk the Kool-Aid, and I didn't like it.

I also didn't like the fact that for Suzuki events my sister took center stage, at least as far as my mother was concerned. These weren't outings focused on me, even though I was the one who first started violin! I was more advanced! I was the one being constantly pressured to practice more!

Once it became clear that my sister and I would continue to progress on the violin, my mother found us a private teacher named Alice, a woman who wound up in our corner of the Hudson Valley from California because she and her soon-to-be-ex-husband were members of the U.S. Army's Strolling Strings ensemble. After a performance at West Point, they looked around the Lower Highlands and decided to settle in tiny servants' quarters at the edge of what had once been an important Cornwall, New York, estate.

All of which fascinated me—and my parents too. Alice and

a few of her friends quickly began playing tennis with Mom and Dad; she was a bit younger than they were but shared their passion for environmental ecology and the northeastern woodlands of the Catskill Mountains. Having never seen my parents be friendly with anyone—my mother didn't even spend much time chatting with her tennis partners—this thaw puzzled but delighted me. I wanted them to spend more time with Alice. I wished Alice would reunite with her ex, John, a very tall and serious man with a thick beard and round gold-rimmed eyeglasses, so that my parents could go on a double date. In middle school, I was obsessed with the rituals of dating and thought that a double date was the height of sophistication.

Maybe, just maybe, if my parents could have a social life, one day I would too.

As I began to moon about boys and dating, my sister's crazed energy was feeding her march through the Suzuki manuals. She didn't mind practicing for hours at a time when she was manic. However, it seemed that only I recognized she was in an altered state. Our parents only saw her liveliness as happiness and her low moods as sadness; "Just part of life," they would say. But I saw something more frightening going on, especially since I was the one hearing her cry at night in our shared bedroom and the one dodging her fists during the day when Dad was at work and Mom was running errands.

One autumn weekend, Alice invited us all to the Carmel, New York, cabin of (more) friends. Everyone was going to play stringed instruments, sing, cook, eat, and take walks. My inherited attention problems combined with my adolescent distractibility had affected my practice. I knew my performance would be bad, and this planed away what little confidence I had. Meanwhile, my sister, buoyed by what I know now to be bipolar mania, jumped in and fiddled with the group despite her youth and ignorance.

Soon she was being toasted with coffee mugs of Blue Nun Riesling and juice glasses of Guinness while I remained in the kitchen with the nonmusicians, chopping vegetables for dinner.

My mother came up behind me as I opened cans of tomatoes. She put her fingers, garlic-scented from stuffing a leg of lamb, on my shoulder. "Don't be jealous of your sister," she said in a surprisingly gentle tone. "This is just her moment. You'll have yours." As usual when my mother offered me comfort, I became sullen, resentful, and closed off. What did she know? Had she ever performed in public? No. Had she ever seen one of her siblings outdo her? No. At that moment, my sister's moment, all I wanted was to be back home, with my books.

In the house where I grew up, books were scarce. That was not because books weren't valued; they were, but it was a different time, and my parents came from backgrounds where books were not valued as possessions. When I was growing up in the 1960s and '70s, books were expensive for lower-middle-class families (and make no mistake, although my father was technically white-collar, his obligations to his ex-wife and sons put us squarely in the blue-collar world financially). Although we had three shelves of books on a hutch in our small living room, they were not highbrow. They included *National Geographic* collections, childcare manuals, home-repair guides, and a few spy thrillers my father collected from airports on business trips.

But it was also because books were scarce in our corner of the world. The nearest bookstore was forty-five minutes away, in New Paltz. The only Barnes & Noble we had back then was nearly two hours away in Manhattan. Borders did not exist. When a shopping mall opened in Newburgh that contained a B. Dalton, I was already sixteen and well accustomed to waiting patiently for books that I could own.

For the children's books my sister and I read, we went to the library, either at our schools or downtown. The real events for me were the monthly orders we placed in our classrooms with Scholastic and the semiannual school book fairs. The former was exciting enough, the careful checks made on the soft newspaper and the awful wait until you got your little bundle of chosen paperbacks held together with a rubber band, but the latter were, for me, an occasion of breathless anticipation. I can still see myself at the first one I attended, held in the combo lunchroom-auditorium of the brand-new school that opened when I was seven years old. Arrayed on table after table in that cavernous space were piles of brand-new books, books that, once purchased, could belong to me. Belong. To. Me.

Anyone who has ever had as many books as she desires from the beginning of life may not be able to fully appreciate the mix of hope and lust in my heart when the doors to that book fair opened. The only restrictions were my reading level and my mother's pocketbook. I was never able to buy all the books I wanted.

However, I felt like the richest girl in the world as I carefully made my selections. *Frog and Toad Together. No Flying in the House. Amelia Bedelia.* Some of these paperbacks, their soft pages now yellowed, still live in our garage, having been read to our daughters after my mother preserved them under the eaves in her house. While my stack of books wasn't always the largest, it was always the one most praised by the teachers tallying the titles up for purchase. "Oh! I love this book," a teacher would say, or "You have chosen some great classics," or "What a good reader you must be to try *Misty of Chincoteague.*"

Their comments and compliments swelled my tiny head, and maybe that was an unmitigated good thing, because I was not a particularly popular kid. Part of this was my predilection for spending time with books instead of people—because people seemed to prefer my quite popular younger sister. She had plenty of friends, plenty of invitations to go and play with other children. She had boundless energy and a willingness to be naughty that I did not possess. If I did something naughty, I worried far too much and too long about the consequences, even if I didn't get caught—and the few times I did misbehave, I always got caught, probably because I was unpracticed. Ellen ran easily with the neighborhood gang in their adventures down by the railroad tracks or across the highway; she laughed loudly, yelled easily, teased mercilessly. The one getting teased was usually me.

I was an ouroboros child, avoiding companionship because I was unpopular, unpopular because I avoided companionship. The only thing that stopped me from swallowing myself whole? Reading. Near-constant reading. If I was reading, I could not hear the voice in my head that recited all my faults to me. *Nobody likes you. You might as well stay inside. You're so fat. You'll never have any friends. All the other kids talk about you behind your back.* I could also quiet the demands from my mother: "You should go outside and get some fresh air. Have you finished your homework? Are you still having trouble with math? You need to practice your violin."

Books provided different voices, and much comfort. I got fresh air from Caddie Woodlawn, made friends with Anne Shirley and Gilbert Blythe, felt liked and approved of by the March sisters. I didn't need to leave my room to experience the Island of the Blue Dolphins, or Blackbird Pond, or the Adirondacks. Every book I read took me away from the confusion of who and where I was. I self-medicated with the best of them, except my substance of choice was "One more chapter!" instead of another sip or toke. But I was as hooked as any junkie.

Fortunately, I could reuse my highs, meaning I could reread my books. As I assiduously curated my small library, I learned to keep the titles that were most delectable and dependable: *A Wrinkle in Time. Fahrenheit 451. Franny and Zooey.* Ibsen's plays. *My Darling,*

My Hamburger. The poetry of e. e. cummings. The two volumes of world literature my mother kept from her community college classes—those were gold, because they contained short stories like de Maupassant's "The Necklace," which I could read again and again.

Losing myself in stories offered the desirable side effect of helping with my grades. Any teacher will tell you that a student who reads is a student who succeeds, a platitude that makes some sense. Some. Avid reading will get you through until you have to think as well as parrot. I didn't read to think, although sometimes the books I read were so powerful I had to (*The Martian Chronicles, Vanity Fair, On the Beach*). I read to escape, to numb, to endure. If I started thinking, I might have to wonder about things or ask questions. Why was my sister so miserable to me? Why did I dislike my father so intensely, to the point of leaving any room he occupied? Why was my mother so miserly yet so intent on sending me to an expensive college? Oh, I had things to think about. I just didn't want to.

Not thinking had its rewards. I'd seen what happened to rebellious teenagers in my mother's family, the ones who dropped out of high school—they got kicked out of the house and had to find work. While I understood that I was being groomed for a different path, I didn't know anyone from my friends' upper-class households who did such things. Everyone my mother steered me toward—"That girl seems to be very serious about the piano. Maybe you could be friends with her?"—had the kind of family that supported its children through college and on to a secure, stable adulthood. If my behavior angered my parents, I might have to leave and find a place to live, get a job, pay my own bills.

I wasn't ready for any of that. I wasn't ready for anything beyond the walls of my bedroom, where I'd pinned up an enormous piece of jungle-themed wallpaper, given to me by the lovely Alice, over the beaverboard and covered it with every photo, ticket stub, magazine tear sheet, and sketch I had. Like every adolescent with her own budding aesthetic, being surrounded by this ephemera simultaneously comforted and energized me.

A violinist for whom I babysat saw how much I loved some of her books and gave me *Amphigorey I* and *II* one Christmas, while Alice introduced me to George Booth's wildly funny, jagged *New Yorker* cartoons. Another classical musician in their circle was married to a professional photographer; their shelves were crammed with more books than I'd ever seen in a private home. Slowly, slowly I saw that there was a world out there that didn't correspond to salaries and the number of bathrooms in a house, a world that was really about how you thought and what you thought about—people actually lived and survived in that world.

But my parents saw that world as scary. "Look at E.'s house!" they'd say, picking me up from babysitting. "She doesn't even have any curtains!" Alice told them stories about how, when times were particularly tough, she and John often subsisted on artist's soup: hot water, ketchup, salt, and pepper mixed together in a Styrofoam cup, all ingredients cadged from a fast-food joint. A pair of vocalists told us they'd gotten through a winter eating just cabbage and rice. That world I was so attracted to? According to my parents, it was a marginal place. "You can't be a writer," they would say, shaking their heads grimly. "Writers don't make enough to pay their bills."

In their world, not being able to pay the bills was the ultimate shame. I don't think my mother ever received a second notice. The minute she received an invoice from a doctor or any other service provider, she was at the table, blue ballpoint in hand, writing a check and placing it in an envelope, stamps at the ready. She balanced that checkbook scrupulously each month; I saw her anguish when something wouldn't add up, usually just a matter of a few dollars.

I didn't understand, as I rolled my teenaged eyes at my mother's bookkeeping, that unlike me, she knew what artist's soup tasted like, aside from its breezy moniker—when it was just something hot that could warm up three kids whose parents hadn't worked for years. She knew how smelly a pot full of cabbage could make a house, which is why she rarely cooked any of her Polish family's recipes. She knew when a friend exclaimed over how hard it had been to deseed currants for a jar of jam that it was even harder to pick those currants in a muggy summer field just so you could have enough money to buy rice and flour. You didn't use that money for books.

Money was always short in our house; if you think because we had a house, because we had enough food, because we had clothing, that it was adequate, think again. When I learned about Maslow's hierarchy of needs in high school, I thought I figured something out, but of course I knew nothing. I thought, *Look at all I am missing!* and missed out on the fact that the Maslow levels are not necessarily building blocks, that you can skip around from one to another and remain injured and broken even while you have a great deal of knowledge.

Maslow identified Level 3 as *Love and belongingness needs*: friendship, intimacy, trust and acceptance, receiving and giving affection and love. Affiliating, being part of a group (family, friends, work).

Somehow, I skipped Belonging and Love Needs and went straight to Esteem.

———

There is often something physically wrong with me. I am, if not a sickly child, a weak one. I'm soft, unmuscular even at my thinnest, and my lungs are constantly straining from asthma and bronchial infections. I get mumps and chicken pox and measles and some sort of rheumatic fever that leaves me unable to walk and my father has to carry me to the car so I can be driven to the doctor's office.

Getting sick is the only time I am given a reprieve from my daily schedule of homework and violin practice and imprecations to "Go get some fresh air." When I am sick, I can lie on the sofa, watch terrible TV, and have my mother serve me soup and ginger ale and the occasional chocolate bar. When I am sick, she ceases what seems to be constant vacuuming. She cares for me instead of just organizing me. Being sick is very sweet.

Being sick also means I don't have to go to school and navigate the maze of social relationships there. Why are some of my classmates popular and others aren't? I'd been taught to be kind to everyone, but it was awfully tough to be kind to the girl who stinks and the boy who steals my homework. I have a lot of allergy problems and am constantly at the nurse's office, coughing and sneezing and scratching my hives. Who wants to be around me? Staying home sick is such a blessing.

Staying home sick also means I get a reprieve from my younger sister's constant noise and movement. When Ellen is around, there is singing and dancing and talking and cleaning and questions and crashing and music. Most unrestful. She follows me everywhere, as younger siblings will, but it doesn't seem to be because she enjoys my company, more because she doesn't want to be without company, because she requires an audience for her hijinks and our mother isn't always available.

In her and my mother's memories I am constantly bossy, trying to round up Ellen and our next-door neighbor friends Sandy and Jackie to play school or newspaper or hospital, but in my memory that's because I need to impose some kind of order on the chaos that threatens to break through whenever Ellen is in charge and we're all forced to dance and sing like dervishes, like her, which exhausts me. My low-lying, completely undiagnosed depression clashed early and often with her childhood mania.

It has taken me decades to understand how other people who

grew up in dysfunctional families, families rife with the kind of abuse I never experienced, could still say "I love my father" or "I love my sister" or aunt or grandparent. Now I do understand. My father has been dead for ten years and I know I love him, know I loved him even when I believed I loathed him. I love my mother. She drives me crazy and I drive her crazy, but we love each other. I also love my sister, although I maintain a distance from her.

I once thought I didn't, because the real friction between me and my three closest family members was partly bad communication—but also partly my constant depression. Those of us who have depression feel numb. We feel hopeless. But part of the disease is not realizing that these feelings are symptoms of the disease. It was absolutely impossible for me to know that at such a young age, in a family that did not acknowledge or understand mental illness despite so many relatives being affected by it. Sure, we had a grandparent living upstairs and several alcoholic uncles, but who doesn't?

No one saw that I was drifting below the normal line, that part of my dreaminess—"You were a child who lived in your imagination," says my mother—had to do with mental illness and not just temperament. I wanted to be left alone because that was easier than trying to make myself understood through the din of other people's needs. My grandmother and my sister needed more help than I did. I can't say I melted into the sidelines. My personality was and is a strong one. But I did try to be left alone as much as possible so I wouldn't have to fight to be heard.

———

When I am in middle school, my mother discovers a music camp in western Massachusetts that she finds suitable for her daughters. Northeast Music Camp no longer exists, but every time I smell pine needles I am instantly transported back to the path leading to the camp dining hall and how we would sing "Peace, I Ask of Thee, O River" each night as a sort of secular compline.

Camp is heaven for a nerdy, violin-playing twelve-year-old. Our counselors all take music very seriously, but most of them are already in college or conservatory and have learned how to tame their geek edges with hipster vibes. They're tanned and cool and really good at music, and our teachers are even better. People practice scales on pine benches in front of our cabins, belt out show tunes on the way to swimming lessons, and noodle over études while sitting on their bunk beds. I make friends—sleepy blond Robin, whose father teaches me voice and loathes my adenoidal pronunciation; energetic Helen, whose cropped hair and peppy conversation will pop up in my dreams decades later; kind and generous Deb, whose family will invite mine on a vacation to Prince Edward Island. I have boyfriends: fast Dave R., shy Chas G., goofy Jeremy S.

I wish I could stay there all summer, maybe even all year, but even if I could, the people I love who make camp what it is would be back with their families in the places where I believe they all feel at perfect ease. Of course, this is not true. They return to families that splinter through divorce, crack with deaths of siblings, explode with secrets revealed. No one's family is perfect, especially when it's not being shaped into a clean narrative for the consumption of camp friends. After we push our footlockers into station wagons and head south along I-95 to homes along the Eastern Seaboard, we each have to acknowledge the gaps and cobwebs in our lives.

But I can't imagine this. I think everyone else's families and houses and lives are pretty much perfect, not because I'm stupid (although I am naïve) but because my parents, really my mother, are so heavily invested in the myth that our family is normal. If my quite-strange family is normal, then other people's families, which are considerably less strange, have to be a lot better off. Jeremy's father is a college rabbi. Deb's parents run an accounting firm to-gether. Helen's family has a summer house. A summer house! I dream about what that might be like, a house where all kinds of relations gather on holidays and a genial rosy-cheeked grandmother cooks large festive meals.

That might be a terribly banal dream. However, I don't yet understand that my dreams might be banal, nor do I understand that when I worry about lacks in my real life I am unknowingly feeding the depression that is already twisted into my brain. It's in-herited, definitely from my father's side of the family and probably from my mother's side too. It's already been given a hearty diet of social isolation, both from my bookish, violin-toting persona and my inability to invite friends over because of my grandmother. If maintaining a healthy social network is one facet of preventing de-pression, I'm several steps behind from the get-go.

During the terribly fraught middle school years, my music-camp friendships sustain me. It's the 1970s, two decades before anyone in my social circle will discover email. We write letters between summer terms, lots and lots of letters on sheets of novelty paper, in which we pour out our hearts the way earlier generations might have written in diaries (we still keep those, too, but our parents are more liberal with money for stationery and stamps). We talk about relationships or lack thereof; musical progress or lack thereof; frustrations with our parents and siblings and school friends. I watch our black metal mailbox like a hawk, knowing that any and every day it might contain a missive to make me feel less alone. The green and yellow and blue and pink envelopes provide a temporary respite from the hours spent on alert in school hallways. Who will notice me? Who will *not* notice me? Who am I supposed to notice? Who am I supposed to ignore? Did I get my hair right?

Rosining up a violin bow can help you produce gorgeous

sounds—if you're well trained, if you know how to play. If you don't, rosin will just help you create screeching din.

One of my camp instructors told me I was going to have a tough time as I progressed and started auditioning for conservatory admission. I looked at him as if he were crazy, because, first of all, who said I was going to audition for music schools?

"Oh, you will be able to," he said. "You're going to be very good. But the problem is, you make it look so easy. When you play, it seems as if you're not working hard at all, and admissions panels dislike that. They prefer a bit of sweat on the brow."

I left that lesson floating on air. I made it look easy! There was something in my life that I did and did well, that I didn't need to be corrected on or urged to do. It was a moment of supreme flow, rare to me, that knowledge you're doing what you should be doing at just the right moment.

5

GRACIOUS LIVING

M Y PARENTS VISIT OUR NEW HOME IN ARLINGTON, Virginia, not long after we've moved in. It's an early autumn day in 2013. After moving from an older home with smaller windows, we're all delighted to sit in the new dining room, sunlight streaming in from the large backyard with its many trees. I've prepared breakfast, the food not fancy, but I've set the table properly, with our flowered cups and plates, pots of jam, platters of fruit and pastries, a butter dish with a butter knife.

My father picks up the latter and turns it over, examining it. "Only snobs use butter knives," he says, and I know he's attempting to be funny but his constant jibes over the years have gotten under my skin.

"Butter knives help keep crumbs out of the butter," I snap back. "They're perfectly practical."

We never had a butter knife growing up. Our sticks of butter and margarine were always full of toast crumbs, globs of jelly, and sometimes bits of baked potato. Having a butter dish was probably fancy to my mother. She may never have seen a butter knife; if she had, she might have decided it was unnecessary, especially with two small children who probably wouldn't use it anyway.

But here I am, forty years old, still waging a cold war with my parents about the choices I've made for my household.

When you're young and spend most of your time with your family of origin, its standards define your world. Of course you eat around the kitchen table and not in a dining room; your small house has no dining room. You don't have a mudroom or an entryway, but you do have a back porch, so you make sure to remove your muddy or snowy boots out there. Shopping for clothes means the clearance rack first and maybe a sale rack after that if there's a special occasion. Steak is served rarely, restaurants an unheard-of treat. These are the rules.

You go out into the world at first by degrees. You meet a school friend whose grandparents treat her to clothes from boutiques, another whose family has a boat, and still another who is allowed to choose her favorite meals twice a week, alternating with her two brothers. You are allowed to choose a favorite meal on your birthday. Otherwise, the days go by on a schedule of foods you don't necessarily like but you're expected to eat without complaint.

A few years later, the clothes, possessions, and activities have become much more disparate. Some classmates have everything trendy; you know that costs a lot of money. Still others, you notice, have different kinds of clothing, not trendy, but obviously expensive and well cared for. Mail-order catalogs have become increasingly popular, so you see some of this kind of garb and know it's too pricey for you to buy or ask your mother to buy.

But it's not just at school or play that you start noticing these differences. Your mother has you involved in myriad activities, including weekly church and its attendant youth group, plus babysitting to make your own money. You start noticing the differences between your house and those of others, differences in furnishings, books, artwork, cooking equipment, even brands of toothpaste. You try things—reading books from the shelves, dabbing on cologne in bathrooms, sometimes (with a friend's permission) trying on and borrowing sweaters, shoes, dresses.

You start to try on different lives, as do all adolescents, but each time you find one that suits you it is beyond your means. You despair. You'll never get there. You'll never escape the claustrophobic feeling of having just enough and no more, and you want more. You want so much more, like Luisa in *The Fantasticks*, whose final screech sends a thrill of recognition up your spine.

Fortunately, your mother secretly wants more, too, mostly for you. So off you go to the expensive private all-women liberal arts college in Massachusetts.

––––

In 1981, we still called the first year of college freshman year, even at Smith, where every student was a girl or a woman (yes, sixteen- and seventeen-year-olds were enrolled). A lot of my freshman year remains a blur, because although I didn't want to acknowledge it, major depression hit early and hard.

Instead, I watched and learned, even as I tried too hard. I tried to bring the right things: a just-tattered-enough poster from the landmark Picasso exhibit at the Met in 1980, a couple of oxford-cloth shirts I'd scored at the Salvation Army, a divided bucket to hold my shampoo and soap for the showers. There were so many things I could not have known to bring. A distressed heirloom steamer trunk. Framed photographs of private-school graduations, girls in white gowns holding long-stemmed red roses. A pile of Fair Isle sweaters. Lilly Pulitzer sheath dresses.

Once a week, at each Smith house (our versions of dormitories, they were supposed to be havens of peace and gentility, but they wound up a cross between convents, sorority houses, and group homes) was a house meeting at which attendance was mandatory unless you were away or at a class. Everyone—from a dozen to a hundred or more students—would gather in the large living room spaces to hear news and chastisements from our head resident, the senior who lived in a suite on the first floor in compensation for her responsibilities.

Smith College once made up part of the Seven Sisters: the seven women's colleges that matched with the Ivy League universities. Smith, Mount Holyoke, Wellesley, Radcliffe, Barnard, Bryn Mawr, and Vassar. (Harvard, Yale, Cornell, University of Pennsylvania, Columbia, Dartmouth, Brown, Princeton.) Today five out of the seven women's colleges remain single sex, although that now also includes women who choose to transition after admission, so there are some male graduates of Smith, Mount Holyoke, Wellesley, Barnard, and Bryn Mawr.

It was radical, in the nineteenth century when these women's colleges were founded, to educate the so-called fairer sex. But no one wanted to be so radical that the status quo might be overturned, so a standard called *gracious living* was sought for America's college girls that would both mimic their upbringings and also equip them for their adult places in society (which, in many cases, meant marriage and family). The vestiges of this idea could still be seen in 1980s Smith houses. We had tea on Friday afternoons, with a cart that held a large pot of black tea, a jug of milk, and a dish of sugar, plus plates of brownies, cookies, and lemon bars. Each Thursday was candlelight supper, with tablecloths and special dishes, and we were encouraged to invite faculty and administration members. Our dining rooms included a set of wooden cubbies into which, after each meal, we rolled (read: stuffed) our personal linen napkins for a week at a time. We didn't need to worry about washing our own sheets unless we wished to, as these were also provided by each house's cleaning person once a week. The flatware was heavy silverware, monogrammed with *SC*.

Sometimes I think back to these days and wonder if I dreamed them. The hall table with its bowl always filled with fresh apples, according to a special alumnae bequest. The house libraries, little warrens of peace and quiet that, during exam periods, filled with the smells of caffeine, nicotine, and flop sweat. The weekend brunches that included choose-your-own omelet stations, giant bowls of fresh fruit salad, and, in the case of Tyler House where I spent three years, an enormous, rich trifle concocted by Chef Isaac, who had been raised in Barbados with its British colonial influences.

It was nothing at all like the way I'd been raised, and I loved it. Of course I did. I'm sure some of my fellow students found it dreary, having been raised in all different kinds of affluent circumstances, but another marker of the 1980s was the number of scholarship students from modest backgrounds, like me, who were admitted to East Coast colleges and universities. While there were students from other underrepresented backgrounds, Black, Latinx, LGBTQIA+, the 1980s were about economic diversity rather than racial equity. My oldest and closest friends from Smith are now mostly quite well off, but several of us came from households with real economic instability. We had to take work-study jobs, we had to apply for loans, and we saved our money carefully, rarely indulging in meals off campus or taking trips that didn't involve buses or rideshares that we found via index cards on a bulletin board in the basement of the library.

It wasn't just about the sweaters or the sterling. It was about the privileged space we all occupied—me, from a downtrodden blue-collar neighborhood in the rust belt alongside Pam from an Upper West Side classic six—that makes a place like a private college special.

The traditions of the school had very little to do with what suited me and everything to do with what I thought was expected of me, what would make me look as affluent as possible. I watched my classmates and housemates carefully, examining their clothes and possessions and habits to glean what I could, what I could afford, what might work for me.

Which is not a new story. Everyone is busy reinventing themselves during adolescence (and way beyond, for that matter). What I didn't understand was that in holding myself to other people's expectations, not only was I reaching for the impossible; I was hurting myself mentally and emotionally.

Being depressed every day—and during high school and college I was not treated for the condition at all—means that every day you come up short. You're not as good, not as worthy, not as savvy, not as talented, not as studious, not as conscientious, not as pretty, not as rich, not as cool, not as, well, almost anything. Depression involves constantly feeling like you're treading water, expending a great deal of energy but not getting anywhere.

The worst part of living by other people's expectations is that you never develop your own.

Who wouldn't want tea on Fridays and weekend brunches? Who wouldn't want a college library filled with treasures and coursework that made you excited, angry, critical, passionate? It sounds as if Smith's expectations of gracious living and gracious thinking were irresistible.

Unless you're depressed, and you can't figure out why. I was surrounded by interesting friends and classmates, given opportunities to travel and work, had a smart and handsome boyfriend—and I still wept in my bed several days of the week.

Because I was well accustomed to living up to other people's expectations, I tried to attach my sadness to whichever of those seemed most relevant. I'm sad because Adam hasn't called today. I'm sad because I got a low grade on my essay. I'm sad because I was too tired to walk downtown and go shopping. I'm sad because Person X doesn't hang out with me very much. I'm sad because I'm homesick.

Until college, I hadn't tied my low moods to specific events. What used to feel like a fog separating me from other people now felt like a black balloon tied to my waist that followed me everywhere. In college, depression felt less confusing and more solid: I was unhappy, period.

I did my best to disguise every inch of my sadness. With some friends and faculty members, I was wholly successful. With others, including the creative nonfiction professor who recommended I read "Creativity and the Neurotic Mind," I was, if not wholly open, completely transparent.

I knew something wasn't right. I had no idea what to do about it. Especially since, having grown very good at functioning, I was pretty sure I wasn't a candidate for any kind of hospitalization. Like all college students, I occasionally drank too much alcohol. I dabbled in weed but preferred to save my money for transportation expenses and new clothes. I didn't have suicidal ideation or actions.

I now know that I was sad. I was depressed, chronically so, even if I was not experiencing major depression. How much of that sadness, however, was inherent, and how much of it was due to my forcing myself into a box as rigid as those wooden napkin cubbies?

From the start of college, I'd wanted to spend my time reading and writing about great literature. Despite my poor performance in my first English course, I got better and better. Not only was I earning As in my English and French literature classes by my senior year; I was also writing for the college newspaper, as well as the literary magazine. One of my creative nonfiction essays was nominated for an award. I had a job offer at a publishing house in Manhattan.

Did I say I didn't know what I wanted? I lied. I knew what I wanted: A life in books. A writing life.

And that terrified me. My mother said that if I wanted to take the job in New York City, I would have to live at home and commute, because of course the salary was very low. She didn't trust me to live with several roommates and manage my finances, and she wasn't wrong. I might have crashed and had to return home anyway.

The thought of going back home to barely make ends meet and live in a house where I wasn't comfortable was awful. I wanted a bigger life, but I didn't know how to make it for myself without the connections some friends had in publishing, at museums, in academia.

I was scared. So scared that instead of looking for a path forward of my own, I decided to hitch my wagon to someone else's star. I was desperately in love with my boyfriend Adam, who was a West Point cadet with a very high GPA and prospects for a bright future in the army. Not many of my classmates were choosing engagement and marriage over jobs and graduate school, but the handful who did made me feel safe and special. The woman who presided over our house dining room gave two of us kitchen witches as bridal shower gifts. One friend and I spent the evening hours of our senior-year spring semester cross-stitching school crests for our fiancés.

My future was certain. My future would not take place in my childhood home. My future would include a wedding, a special military-spouse passport, and a move across the ocean. I thought I would never be sad again.

6

LIFE DURING WARTIME

WELCOME TO BERLIN 1986, A DIVIDED CITY IN A divided country. We live in the American-controlled suburb of Zehlendorf at the southwest corner of West Berlin, completely surrounded by a border known as The Wall, *Die Mauer*. Everyone knows what it is; far fewer know what it's like to be there. It's at once too big and too small, one hundred miles of post–World War II Allied political territory that contains as many tiny gossipy villages as rural Arkansas yet also maintains enough cultural sophistication to rival New York, London, Paris, and more.

West Berlin makes me ache with excitement and sob with loneliness.

———

Adam and I arrived at Berlin Tegel on Super Bowl Sunday after an overnight flight with a stop in Frankfurt that neither one of us registered as we slept on each other's newlywed shoulders.

One of Adam's new fellow lieutenants picked us up and took us to meet another lieutenant at a down-market Chinese restaurant where the most exotic thing I tasted was the Spezie, a mixture of Coke and Fanta. Both young men must have talked to me, must have asked me how the flight was, must have made some kind of conversation, but all I remember is their work chatter with Adam: who he needed to meet, what the weekly battalion schedule was, where his tank company was located. I rested my head on one hand and twirled the straw in my soda, my traveling hat on the seat beside me along with my dreams of European glamor. We had entered The American Zone.

Amerikanische Berlin (one of the only German phrases the lieutenants knew and taught me was how to say "Ich bin Amerikanerin") comprised the city's wealthiest enclaves, Zehlendorf and Dahlem, filled with green spaces, mansions, tony restaurants, and important institutions, including the Freie Universität. Since that school was a matter of minutes from American headquarters, I was sure I'd able to audit some classes, make some friends, hang out at a few cool cafés.

Brad, the lieutenant assigned to take care of us, drove us down tree-lined streets to the Dahlem Guest House, a hostel owned by the U.S. government as temporary housing. Brad, visibly relieved to leave us and go back to his apartment to nurse his Super Bowl hangover, gave Adam a card with the phone number of his new company commander and took off in his BMW.

The lobbies on each floor of the guest house were filled with an assortment of women and children in various states of disarray—babies nursing, mothers chasing toddlers, ladies in curlers smoking and drinking mugs of what I hoped was coffee but could just as easily have been bourbon. A German attendant walked us to our third-floor room and opened the door onto a narrow cell containing a double bed, a sink, a desk chair, and a plywood wardrobe with a TV perched on top. Adam saw my eyes go wide but gave the attendant a tip and put down our suitcases (most of our luggage and other things would arrive in a few weeks via steamship).

When the door closed, I hissed, "What *is* this? We can't stay here! This is worse than an Econo Lodge! Are you sure they know you're an officer? Maybe this is where they put the enlisted families."

That young woman was spoiled and overprivileged and entitled and narrow-minded and ignorant, but also confused, sad, and shipwrecked, fighting a battle that no one else saw.

———

Just a few weeks after Adam and I arrive in West Berlin, we're living in an apartment. My first home. Well, it's really Adam's first home; I'm living in it because I am Family Member 01, Dependent Spouse.

I had no intention of becoming an officer's wife. Growing up close to the United States Military Academy made me actively wary of becoming one, since I saw many of the young women who did. Theirs was not the life I wanted.

Yet here I was, married to a West Pointer. As recent college graduates, Adam and I owned very little besides our clothes; my parents gave me a small table and a rocking chair that had belonged to Grandmother Collier. We had some wedding gifts, many almost cruelly impractical, like curlicue-chased silver-plated pastry tongs. We had books and a few *New Yorker* covers that I framed and hung in our living room. Some of our friends from high school and college were putting books and *New Yorker* covers into much smaller apartments in Manhattan, Chicago, San Francisco, Washington, D.C.; we had a large two-bedroom with a roomy balcony.

I loved it, and I hated it. I loved it because it belonged to us. There was no grandmother upstairs or downstairs, no sister sharing my bathroom, no roommate or friend asking to borrow things. I could leave all my clothes in a heap. I could let the dishes pile up in the sink. I could fill the refrigerator with bottles of wine and hunks of good cheese. Our funky German bathroom had a big tub and a huge medicine cabinet. I was playing house. We were playing house. We might as well have been two little Fisher-Price plastic people, inserted into this apartment by a giant toddler. We were no more at home in this first apartment than dolls.

And that's why I hated it too. Like 1960s playsets, our life together fell strictly along gender lines. Each morning, the boy doll woke early and headed to his tank company for PT, or physical training, the round of two-mile run, push-ups, and sit-ups that U.S. Army soldiers everywhere do. The girl doll slept later, then wondered what to do with her day besides cook the dinner that would be the only meal the boy doll ate at home. She was invited on girl-doll outings, trips to IKEA for Billy bookcases and "fun" kitchen towels, excursions downtown for *Kaffee und Küchen* in shopping districts. He was building his career and learning how to be a soldier, while she was stocking their linen closet and learning how to order ladies' lunches *auf Deutsch*.

If that disparity wasn't an occasion for depression, I don't know what would have been. At least for me. My friends from Smith were learning the ropes at their jobs on Wall Street, or getting excited about grad school seminars, or teaching their first AP History classes; none of them, not a single one, even the other two who had gotten married quickly, sat at home sewing curtains. I'd had two job offers—not lucrative ones, because they were in publishing, but I'd had them. I'd left those jobs behind in order to take this journey with Adam.

———

The American Military Hospital in Berlin offered mental health counseling. The only other time I'd been to the hospital was the week we moved into our apartment, when I accidentally burned my hand on our brand-new coffee maker.

A doctor in an army uniform assessed my burn, which was second degree and required a pot of shiny white ointment that eased the ache. If the hospital could take care of my hand, maybe they could also take care of my mind. I made an appointment and called in to see a plump blond German woman in a bright-blue wool dress named Helga.

Helga sounded friendly. I told her I was sad. So sad. I might have done the wrong thing by getting married. I missed the United States. I wanted a job, a career, and I was not sure I could fit in with the military community.

Helga said, "I am sure you are lonely, but to fix this is a simple matter. You should join a group. Take up a hobby! Things are not so bad as they seem, Mrs. Patrick."

I wanted to explain that I was called Ms. Kelly, but I decided not to waste too much time of the scant five sessions family members were allowed with counselors at that time. I said, "I am not much of a joiner. I liked to read, and write, and travel. I want to make some friends, but maybe some German friends, people at the university."

"Splendid!" Helga slapped her bright-blue-clad thighs. "There is a very fine American-German Friendly Society where you can meet all types of Berliners."

I knew about the American-German Friendly Society, and I knew that it was made up of people ten and twenty years older than me. I didn't know how I would fit in. I never attended a meeting, and while I did go to my four remaining appointments with Helga and continue to tell her I was very, very sad, she never offered any advice or counsel other than "Keep looking for new things to do. That is, I know, the best way to compensate for your state of loneliness."

There is chemical depression that stems from brain dysfunction, and there is situational depression that stems from outside stressors. At this point in my life I'd had family-of-origin dysfunction. Now I was having family-of-choice dysfunction. I'd chosen to marry

Adam. I'd chosen to move across the ocean with him. I'd chosen to become a military spouse.

My choices. I wasn't a woman who had been pushed into early marriage. If I had wanted to, I could have taken a job and made my slow, painful way into adult life, like so many of my college friends were doing, sharing apartments with five roommates and subsisting on buttered noodles. When people ask me now why I got married so young, I usually smile and dip my head and say, "I fell in loooooove," to make them laugh and stop myself from boring them with all the fallout: That I was frightened I could not make it on my own. That I was desperately in love but also attracted to other men. That I envied my friends who were smarter, more ambitious, less fearful. That I longed to get away from my family.

I knew I was prone to depression, but I didn't think about how my bluesy temperament might interact with a situation like being an army wife in a walled city. How could anyone be so naïve? I was. I was so awed by the glamor of a ready-made identity that I jumped without glancing ahead, my satin wedding dress a parachute. Married, I would have health insurance. Married, I would have plans for each day, week, month, year. Married, I would not have to explain myself to anyone. Married, I would have a self.

———

The 1980s American military: don't ask, don't tell, don't even speculate. Berlin has always been an edgy city where every kind of lifestyle can be accommodated.

Educational films warned us that many things, not just homosexuality, could be leveraged for bribery. After I was lucky enough to get a job at the U.S. Command, Berlin Headquarters (quaintly housed in the former Nazi-built Luftwaffe Headquarters), I regularly walked its clinical halls with all manner of intelligence officers: army, navy, State Department, CIA, NSA . . . I was, of course, almost entirely ignorant of who was whom, although I did recognize that having an office for the navy in landlocked Berlin was probably a smoke screen.

I needed a lot of correction, but I rarely received it about the right things, let alone from the right people.

The woman in the office next to mine told me, after Adam had gone to great lengths to replace my college ring, that wearing it on my middle finger (he'd had it sized too big) made me look like a hippie.

———

I had to draft a new regulation about cigarette smoking in government offices by myself. Months later, I found a marked-up copy in our file cabinet, a tornado of red-pen corrections headlined with the statement "I was not responsible for this work" in my colleague's hand.

Nonmilitary American friends who regularly used our apartment to do their laundry or cook meals complained that I didn't sharpen my knives properly, and why didn't I have potato starch in my pantry?

The hospital nutritionist said I needed to lose at least twenty pounds and that to do so I would need to exercise twice a day and restrict myself to a thousand calories per day.

Adam's battalion commander didn't like my attitude during Adam's promotion ceremony to first lieutenant. The commander, a lieutenant colonel, ordered us both into his office and forced us to listen to a tirade about loyalty. Directed to me: "I'm trying to teach your husband to go to *war*, Bethanne!"

Who was teaching me about what to do while my husband learned to go to war? All I'd gleaned so far was the trick of freezing a tray full of prescooped sherbet in dishes so that a large dinner-party dessert could be served quickly. No one spoke to me about how to live by myself for weeks and sometimes months at a time while the battalion trained. No one discussed where we were supposed to go if a bomb hit the post exchange or the Burger King. No one asked, "What do you want from your life?" because, it was assumed, you'd already figured that out by marrying into the military.

I did not slip further into depression in Berlin because I was an entitled nitwit. I slid further into depression in Berlin because I was losing my identity before I even figured out what it was. Yes, I needed to learn how to support my husband and to modulate my sense of humor when it pertained to his career. Yes, I needed to understand that officers did not and should not live in luxury, and I needed to understand that an expensive liberal arts education was not the sole measure of a person's worth.

However, that was the only measure that counted in my previous world. It would take me a few years and countless missteps before I had the humility and understanding to truly connect with some of the other men and women serving in Berlin. But it would take me many years, in fact a few decades, to realize the system we were all serving in was flawed.

————

I wasn't a warrior, by anyone's standards. But I heard gunfire off in the distance, from Allied exercises, from Iron Curtain exercises, from East German guard drills. There were lots of parades, the kind of puffery armies engage in to assure one another of their existence. Before each major parade—Fourth of July, May Day, Armistice Day, others—Adam and his fellow Armor Company service-members would spend hours and hours cleaning their tanks and carefully buffing them with baby oil, the better to make them shine as they caught the morning sun along the roads of the Tiergarten.

Always ready. We lived closer to Poland and the Soviet Union than we did to West Germany. We believed we lived on the brink of nuclear war. We were told we lived on the brink of nuclear war and experienced near-constant anxiety about what would happen and where we would go if it occurred. All of us were tense, wired for emergency, afraid to be less than perfect in case we were judged by superiors, or peers, or the actual Berliners who lived their lives for decades under occupation.

Living in a state of near-constant anxiety can cause post-traumatic stress disorder (PTSD). I do not want to diminish the experience of anyone who has lived through violent combat or disaster, nor do I want to co-opt the experience of trauma victims with Complex PTSD (a very serious and different disorder). But just as there are different levels of depression, I believe there are different levels of PTSD—and everyone I know who lived in West Berlin, behind The Wall, coped with anxiety and PTSD of some kind.

There was the man who ran miles every weekend, even when his wife begged him not to because weekends were the only times he could be home. The woman who, after returning from West Berlin, scratched her throat obsessively until it scabbed. My junior-high social studies student (I spent a happy if frazzled year teaching at Berlin American High School) who asked if the school had an air-raid shelter. Officers' wives who hoarded Hummel figurines and KPM china sets and even Hermès scarves from the French military exchange. Fears and worries and obsessions.

We were all affected.

––––

Listen for the rumble as it grows nearer, an unmistakable mechanical whir. Part the heavy brown curtains. Crank open the casement window and lean out as far as you can without jackknifing over the sill. When the tanks reach your block, begin waving maniacally, especially when you spot your husband's helmeted head. He's the tank commander and also the platoon commander, shepherding his bulky dark-green-treaded sheep from their nearby headquarters to their inner-city training fields.

WE LIVED IN a city where tanks of several nations regularly rolled down cobblestoned streets. We lived in a city with a Bomb Threat Report Form on the cover of our telephone book. We lived in a city that required us to take a special train if we wanted to get out from behind the Iron Curtain to visit the free world. We lived in a city rife with spies and surveillance, but also within a community rife with class inequity and nasty backbiting. Were you in more danger leaving the American Sector or remaining within its boundaries?

I knew that leaving the borders of West Berlin illegally wasn't in any way a good idea, but I also knew that while I was there, I would not be able to grow and change the way I wanted to, that there were borders within borders, boundaries within boundaries, that kept me separate from the people whose ideas and work interested me most. I don't blame myself for not knowing precisely who those people were. I was only twenty-two when we arrived in Germany, twenty-five when we left. But somewhere deep inside I understood that our Berlin community wasn't my community.

7

THE GINKGO PATH

ADAM GENTLY PUT THE TELEPHONE RECEIVER BACK in its cradle—our Berlin telephone was a big beige block, a rectangle of German efficiency that we received, like everyone else, through the Bundesrepublik—and turned to embrace me in a fierce hug. He had just learned he'd been accepted into the U.S. Army's Funded Legal Education Program, which meant he could go to law school free of charge, with a salary, as long as he remained in the military for six years afterward.

It also meant I could enroll in graduate school for English literature, my big dream. We both believed then that our real lives were beginning.

I hadn't been the only one frustrated by our life in Berlin. Although Adam had chosen Armor Branch while still at West Point, it was more because he didn't want to be in the infantry or field artillery, yet he'd had it drummed into him that a combat-arms branch was the best route for promotion.

But tanks are greasy and noisy and smelly. They didn't capture Adam's rather academic imagination. He'd won a political science award upon graduation, and here's what I thought the plan was: Adam would complete his mandatory five years of military service, perhaps spending a couple of them getting a master's degree in political science or international relations. After that, he'd be a civilian on the way to a doctorate and a tenure-track position at a lovely small college somewhere in a temperate climate. Eventually I'd finish a doctorate, too, after having a few children, and we'd both aspire to administrative positions, perhaps deanships. We'd have interesting hobbies. I was ready to pick up my violin again, or maybe trade it for a viola da gamba as I had briefly in college, or even keep up my classical voice lessons; maybe Adam would start fly-fishing.

––––––

Moves are stressful, whether prompted by military service or not, but they are also busy, purposeful, and process driven. On landing, we parked our suitcases with my parents and drove down to Virginia to find a house. Back to New York State to buy some inexpensive furniture and to refinish some freebies from family. Then south to Charlottesville, where we'd soon discover how much tighter our budget was with one salary instead of two without the military commissary.

I started my first semester with brio, eager to attend each session of each class, especially the one to which I'd been assigned as a grader—the graduate student who is responsible for marking all exams and papers the professor assigns. By November, I was helplessly sobbing on the secondhand sofa in our townhouse, praying that I'd either be brave enough to kill myself or have the kind of stroke that turns you into a savant.

What happened? Was this a storm or an entirely new microclimate that would remain in place for years?

––––––

We've all heard the phrase *Fake it till you make it*. I tried. Oh, I tried. I showed up for group coffee chats and dropped as many names and

ideas as I could. I moaned with friends about our reading load and
the lack of materials for a set of assigned essays, propped my feet
up in the tiny department reading room filled with the entire Loeb
Classical Library, and drank the downright egregious grad/faculty
lounge coffee made in a Bunn machine.

Then I would go home, sit on the awful sofa, and cry and cry
and cry. Something was terribly wrong, and I knew it; you don't
cry that hard and not know something is wrong. It's the kind of
crying that induces lachrymal hangovers—headaches and dehydra-
tion and existential dread. I would get up each day and take the
same path to the library, a gentle incline that would, each fall, become partially covered in the leaves and then the berries of female
ginkgo trees that smelled like vomit.

———

In order to understand how and why I fell into what was at least my
second and possibly third major depression, you have to understand
a little about the late-1980s University of Virginia English Department's winnowing process. It stunk as badly as the ginkgo berries.
Each year, UVA English would admit up to eighty master's degree
candidates, requiring three semesters of classes and either passing an
oral exam or writing a thesis. During the third semester, master's
candidates were allowed to go up for permission as doctoral candidates. Only twenty members of any master's class received this
permission.

We knew we couldn't, wouldn't, all make it. Whispers abounded.
She's hopeless at scansion. He has no idea what he's talking about
when he talks about Faulkner. Did you hear the ridiculous the-
ory he's spouting on Kristeva? It doesn't matter how many times
she goes to Mr. D.'s office hours; she's never going to be anything
more than a solid B student. In the low-ceilinged corridors of Wilson Hall (since demolished; the halls were probably rife with black

mold), we plotted and schemed against each other with the fervor of Borgias and Tudors.

An unhealthy environment, even for the absolute stars who were mentally healthy and highly functioning individuals. For someone like me, mentally ill and with an unstable personality, it was a bubbling cauldron of despair and self-doubt.

I had absolutely no idea that there might be something classifiable about my problems with academic work. If only someone—my parents, a teacher, another adult—had recognized my disorganization and last-minute completion of work for what it was. Attention deficit disorder was not coined or defined until 1980, which might have been right on time had I not already developed dozens of coping strategies to hide the disability I didn't want anyone else to see (which, of course, meant that probably everyone was well aware of it).

The problem was I didn't realize it was a disability; I thought it was just the way my brain worked and that there was nothing to be done about it. Most of my academic needs were kept in my head—lists of French verbs, the American presidents in chronological order, memorized poems, homework bullet points.

Not being able to sustain thoughts has disastrous effects on graduate work of any kind but particularly in the humanities, where you're supposed to sustain thoughts about other people's thoughts. I was twenty-six, and ADD interfered with my ability to do the work I'd signed up to do—that inability, and my awareness of it, pushed me over the edge from low and enervated to desperate and trapped.

One of my fellow students in the Old English class invited me to his place for a cram session. As the hours passed, it became clear that I hadn't done enough work—hadn't been able to do the work. We reviewed conjugations and translations; I put my head in my hands and began to cry as I had so many times that month, but this time in surrender. I gave up.

———

Another fall in Charlottesville, but now it's 1996, and as I stride up the odiferous ginkgo-covered sidewalk to Alderman Library, there's a smile on my face. I'm heading to the reference room to claim a seat at one of the round tables I prefer and spend the next six hours engaged in research on my thesis.

There is nothing like having a child to wonderfully concentrate the mind. Our daughter Emma is almost four years old, a perfect, healthy, beautiful hellion whose every move requires supervision. Leave her alone for five seconds and find her covered in yogurt, five minutes and pray that she hasn't run off with someone on a bicycle. We have her enrolled in a Montessori school within walking distance of the house we'd bought while Adam was still in law school, the house we were again living in, back in C-ville for a year while he completed his military LLM at the Judge Advocate General School.

When we'd returned, in early June, I was still experiencing the major depression into which I'd fallen after a second-trimester miscarriage. A large part of Emma's bad behavior had to do with a mother who had checked out mentally. I went through the motions, packing lunches for day excursions, decorating her bedroom, filling out forms for preschool, but I could barely function. At every opportunity I lay down for naps, the oblivion of sleep my only drug—we didn't drink much, and even if I'd liked a uncontrolled substance, I wouldn't have known where to find it.

Fortunately, when we returned for an appointment with the doctor who had delivered Emma, he recognized my mental illness had returned and immediately urged me to get back on Prozac. By mid-July, I was back—still no ball of fire, but at least I cared about living and wanted to engage with my husband and child.

I also cared about what I was going to do during the days while Emma went to school and on playdates and Adam drove up to the JAG School for classes. The ten-month academic year was too short for me to get any sort of meaningful job, and we knew we wanted to try for another baby, so neither of us wanted me to take on anything too stressful. I pondered these puzzles until, one day while meeting an old friend for coffee at The Mudhouse on Charlottesville's Downtown Mall, I learned about the Jefferson Scholars Program. Part of the university's Continuing Education arm, this program allowed former degree holders to come back and design a semester of their own in support of further study or a profession.

Writing a thesis gave shape and purpose to days that otherwise might have left me back in the formless days like those I'd known after I finished my master's coursework. What do you do when a door slams shut and no window appears to be open? Depends on your temperament—and your frame of reference. I didn't want to teach high school, public or private; that felt like settling for scraps. I thought about freelance writing, but I didn't know how to start.

———

In 1996 I was back in Life B, on Prozac, after an interlude for pregnancy and childbirth and new parenthood and a move to Texas and a move back from Texas and a miscarriage and a deep major depression. I was stable again, my daughter enrolled in preschool, my husband occupied with coursework, and me set up with our extra bedroom as a home office, complete with the clunky beige PC, clunky beige printer, and electric kettle so I could make tea without the distraction of going downstairs to the kitchen.

Returning to Charlottesville suited us, and yes, we both understood that our privileged life there was made possible by outside forces, but we had to ignore them for a while. We'd earned a breather, and we took it. I made new doctors' appointments, stocked a new pantry with fresh spices and condiments, and enrolled Emma in various classes and play groups.

EACH SUNDAY ADAM would drop me off at the sidewalk across from my ginkgo path so I could spend the entire afternoon engaged in research. He and Emma would head home to change and then walk to a park near our house that provided all the swing sets and bouncy horses she required to burn off her considerable energy. By that time in the week I'd exhausted all my efforts at the same, and Adam knew it. Diving into the cool air of Alderman Library became my escape from the humid atmosphere of parenting the world's busiest four-year-old girl.

As a continuing education student I could not be assigned a library carrel, which meant I had to tote whichever books I needed from my home office along to the reference room each week, but this was a small price to pay for my six hours of freedom in the library.

The Prozac coursing through my veins allowed me enough mood stability to keep my worst distractibility in check. It also allowed me to close books after I'd gotten what I needed and return my focus to the perhaps slimmer and more complex texts that were most vital to my thesis. Thinking more clearly was an even greater relief than being spelled for a time on parenting.

I hadn't let my mistakes define me. I read and read and read, marveling at how much easier it was to keep the sentences and paragraphs distinct while medicated. I still did not know about attention deficit disorder at all, let alone its adult onset. All I knew was that what once had been garbled was now clear.

———

That year in Charlottesville was a gift, a blessing after the sadness of miscarriage and the swamp of depression that followed. Each week followed a rhythm: Adam to school, Emma to school, me to the library and study. Emma had playdates and a wonderful fourth birthday party at a little children's museum. We saw family for Thanksgiving and Christmas. The pages of my thesis began to stack up in a meaningful way.

As I racked up days in the library, I started to hope, in a very small way, that I might use this work as a springboard to enter a doctoral program. We knew that after law school, Adam's next assignment would be at the Pentagon, just a couple of hours away from Charlottesville. Perhaps I could spend a day or two each week away from home, completing coursework. Emma would be in Montessori kindergarten. We could get a part-time nanny.

But Adam wanted another baby. "We have the heir; let's have the spare!" he cajoled me. I hmphed, hemmed, and hawed. I didn't want to throw away my shot at a PhD. Really, I was terrified that I might miscarry again. I didn't think my psyche could handle another pregnancy loss, even if I was now in the land of obstetricians and psychiatrists who understood that not all antidepressants crossed the placenta, doctors who believed that the mother's mental health was just as important as her physical health in seeing a healthy pregnancy to term.

———

By February 1997 we observed the blue line on the drugstore test. By March I'd convinced our beloved OB that I should receive an early ultrasound. I knew that I needed to hear a heartbeat. The OB scheduled the test and reminded me that if there were any questions from the technician or our insurance that I was to tell them I'd seen some spotting. He understood my paralyzing fear, knew that I couldn't go on without some reassurance.

Adam and I knew that with a second baby on the way I was unlikely to pursue further study. We'd be moving, we'd have two young children, I'd find something else to do, and so on. Unfortunately a lot of the "and so on" came not from me but again from Adam. "You don't need a PhD. It's a waste of time and money, and besides, there are no jobs in academia. Don't bother with that; you can find something else to do."

His comments made some sense, but not to my heart. I was pregnant, but I was also still researching, reading, and writing. Sometimes I nodded off at my chosen reference-room table, the flood of first-trimester hormones overwhelming me, but after a brief nap I woke up ready to return to making notes on *The Rule of Saint Benedict* and the vocabulary changes in my tenth-century text.

I scheduled my thesis defense for June. Since I wasn't required to hold a defense, it made the most sense to ask the professors involved to work with me once their final exams and grading were finished. Here's where those pregnancy hormones gave me an advantage. In some women with treatment-resistant depression, pregnancy and the postpartum fourth trimester are a time free from low moods, a time of remarkable stability. Scientists aren't sure exactly which hormone cocktail makes this possible, but for me and other pregnant depressives, it's a heady combo. I felt better during my two complete pregnancies than I ever did otherwise, despite the usual morning sickness, fatigue, and other indignities of the state (heartburn, joint pain, hemorrhoids—oh, the glamor!). I glowed with mental health.

So I had an amazing experience defending my thesis to both my advisors, who signed off on it and presented me with an A. I wasn't sure what I was going to do next, besides give birth (my baby was now a very healthy five months along), but I knew I was no longer a person incapable of academic work.

We found a house to rent in Arlington, Virginia. A Montessori kindergarten for Emma, a pediatrician, a dentist, and a psychiatrist who also offered talk therapy. The next two years were so happy.

In November I had a beautiful baby girl, Martha. An old friend, a teacher, helped me get some freelance work.

So when Adam came home in early 1999 and told me he'd been selected for Command and General Staff College at Fort Leavenworth, Kansas, I was less than thrilled. But I was blindsided, and I think that was also part of my depression. More than once in our marriage I had engaged in purely magical thinking. First it was believing that my new husband would leave the military as soon as possible and enter academia. Then it was believing that my attorney husband would support my academic dreams. Next, I believed that we would move to and stay in a place that could sustain some sort of professional life for me while we raised our children.

Depression told me, and kept telling me, to rely on someone else. Depression told me that I was not enough, that I could not pursue my dreams within my framework but only within the strictures of my marriage to an army officer. Even though I occasionally wept at the idea of falling in love with someone else or considered staying behind while Adam moved, those options were as featherlight to me as the idea that I might actually succeed within the confines I had.

———

Did my choices deepen my depression? Or did my depression affect my choices? Even if the answer is both, it's more complicated than that. By 1999 I'd experienced three major depressions. Since I didn't understand that I was still depressed, I didn't know enough to ask my psychiatrist for a change of medication or a new approach to stress reduction. If my first few years on Prozac had offered a wonderfully clear new world, now I was in a weird sort of holding pattern.

Other women in the civilian world, I slowly realized, had help from nuclear and extended families, nannies and au pairs, housecleaners and gardeners. But in the closed world of military families on set salaries, stay-at-home spouses, and less of a support network, wives were still expected to handle it all—and to handle it with aplomb. "God's Grace Will Not Send You Where God's Love Will Not Carry You" read a needlepoint sampler on the wall of one friend's home. In many others: "Bloom Where You Are Planted." I got the message.

The trouble was, I wasn't interested in any of the things my fellow military spouses seemed to love, whether Pampered Chef and Longaberger Basket parties or bunco nights or working out at the gym while the kids were in school. When we arrived at Fort Leavenworth, couples were invited to the auditorium at Bell Hall for an address by the Command and General Staff College commandant. He urged us all to attend our neighborhood bible-study groups in order to foster our faith and our community.

Adam, ever a joiner, said we should go; I preferred to keep my faith separate from my community, thank you very much. It struck me then, hard, that I was in the wrong tribe. I had no idea, at that point, where my own tribe was except in Bryant Hall at the University of Virginia—and it didn't seem I would get back there any time soon.

8

—

DISRUPTIVE

THE THICKSET WOMAN IN A FLOWERED SMOCK LOOKED at me impassively as she stood in the church parking lot to lower the boom: my eight-year-old daughter would not be allowed to return to her Brownie troop meetings.

"She's disruptive," said troop leader Bonnie. "None of the other girls get anything done when she's around."

I glanced over my shoulder, hoping the daughter in question, Emma, and her three-year-old sister, Martha, couldn't hear Bonnie from the backseat of our Ford Explorer. Probably not; they were singing along to "Your Body Is a Wonderland." I was sure Bonnie didn't approve of this musical choice any more than she did of my daughter's behavior. But what did I care? I was stuck in the middle of central Texas with two wriggly children, and if they preferred John Mayer to Raffi I was not going to argue. I needed to save my battles for the times when they weren't secured by seatbelts and entranced by Top 40 music.

When I was growing up, the Girl Scouts of the U.S.A. was a family religion. My mother spent seven years as leader of my sister's and my Junior Scout troop, and she and my father spent later years on the local Girl Scout council as well. Ellen and I loved everything about scouting, from our Brownie beanies to our badge-filled sashes. I stayed in through Cadets and would have been a Senior Girl Scout if a troop had existed. Being a Girl Scout was wholesome, edifying, and achievement-oriented: my mother's trifecta.

Today I understand I have attention deficit disorder. I know that from my earliest recollections I had difficulty concentrating on one thing at a time, finishing what I started, and making decisions, all hallmarks of ADD and its sister challenge ADHD (attention deficit hyperactivity disorder).

Girl Scouting was the mid-twentieth-century antidote for ADD. Each chapter of the *Girl Scout Handbook* was a lesson not just in a topic but in how to break that topic down into steps to match different kinds of learning styles. You had something to read, something to do, something to hear or watch or find. And then there were the badge requirements! If you followed the instructions and checked off the items on a list, you earned a tiny, pretty embroidered patch to sew onto your sash or vest. Along with the jewel-toned badges, you could earn bigger patches by attending events, like a camporee or Thinking Day Fair.

Our sashes were marvels of precision, both in earned badges and in our mother's precise stitching. She didn't love sewing, but she knew how to sew plainly and well, her heavy 1960s Pfaff Dial-A-Stitch machine a point of pride. Years later, after inheriting it, I decided to sell it for seventy-five dollars to a grad school classmate who wanted to be able to stitch her own tent; my mother was outraged that I could let it go, not because she considered it an heirloom but because it was such a fine machine. "You don't see that kind of steel anymore," she said.

Being a troop leader required a similar kind of steel. For seven years Mom and her coleader Susan M. spent every Wednesday afternoon and many weekends wrangling as many as two dozen little girls through wriggly recitations of the Girl Scout Promise, craft projects that covered everyone in Elmer's Glue and tempera paint, and the much-longed-for snack time.

During the 1970s, Girl Scout leaders were mostly upper-middle-class alpha moms, and even though our family slouched in a trough of lower-middle-class budgetary despair, my mother was determined to hoist us all up through every means of voluntarism possible. She served on the town council. She was our neighborhood's American Heart Association donation solicitor. She ran the nearby Teen Center for several years, devoting weekday evenings after her young children were put to bed to making sure older kids had somewhere safe to go. She taught after-school tennis clinics and went on field trips as a chaperone. She threw her considerable energy and intelligence into all the activities that would keep her on the high side of respectability, all the activities that kept her as different from her family of origin as possible.

Some of these stories will make my mother sound hard and controlling. She *is* hard and controlling. She was unyieldingly stern to her own mother, brusque to the point of rudeness to her mother-in-law, and businesslike in the face of her only sister's poverty-stricken life.

Yet she is also loyal and generous. She allowed her mother to live with us for nearly fifteen years, visited her mother-in-law every week for twelve years, and saw her sister weekly until that sibling's cancer forced her to move in with my parents until death.

Those three figures in my mother's life are dead. My sister and I are very much alive. To us she was hard and controlling, loyal and generous, stern and brusque and businesslike and whimsical and kind and patient. Like all mothers, she was and is a bundle of contradictions, some of which make perfect sense and others which will forever be mysterious to me.

My mother's heart, that complicated muscle, remains strong and vital.

———

By the time my daughter is old enough for Brownies, the Girl Scouts of the U.S.A. has changed a great deal, in many good ways—more diverse troops, more troops in urban areas, more attention to socially relevant issues and less time spent on embroidery—and in a few bad. Fewer and fewer women with education and ambition want to spend their time receiving no pay and few accolades. "Girl Scout leaders are blue-collar women now," a friend with older children tells me, and while I wince at the classism in that comment, I see that my daughter's Brownie leaders Bonnie and Linda are different than my mother and Susan M. Mom and Mrs. M. had simple pageboy hairstyles, drove station wagons, and read *Good Housekeeping*; Bonnie and Linda wear polyester, drive trucks, and bring in copies of *US* and *People* for the girls' collages.

Emma's ouster from Brownies was a catalyst for me as a parent. If she couldn't even handle an after-school activity, one that I knew she basically enjoyed, I needed to get help figuring out why.

But the troop leader's words were not the first clue we'd had that Emma was different. A bright child who spoke at three months, walked at nine months, and made her first joke somewhere in between, she was also a hurricane whose constant activity and lack of naps kept me exhausted. She caused a sensation in Montessori school by gathering her five-year-old cohorts in the coatroom and explaining how babies got into mommies' *'chinas*. On the short walk home from her elementary school (where she'd been put directly into first grade), she would take off her socks and boots and tread barefoot in the snow, assuring our chaperoning neighbor that her feet liked the cold.

Yes, she was smart. But she was also impulsive and angry and wildly energetic. When she was around eighteen months, I took her to the Fort Hood hospital for a routine checkup. The doctor, who was Turkish, spoke with a heavy accent. He said something that I assumed I misheard.

"The mailman goofed," he repeated and smiled at Emma, who was attempting to climb over his shoulder so she could get down from the table. "He put the boy letter in the girl box." It was his way of saying that my daughter was hyperactive.

But that was as far as it went for several years. Adam laughed and called our daughter "devil girl" when she acted out or refused to listen. He delighted in her naughty behavior, perhaps because he'd been allowed so little of it in his own childhood, growing up with a very strict mother and maternal grandmother. He told me to stop worrying so much about her defiance and impulsivity, but he wasn't the one who witnessed her in the company of other children. When I took her to the park, to birthday parties, I saw that other toddlers and preschoolers listened to mundane instructions from their mothers like "Finish your juice before you leave the table" and "Share that toy with the others." When I picked Emma up to leave and she didn't want to go, she would punch me repeatedly in the neck and face. "Don't hit your mother, sweetheart," one friend told her. From the look on Emma's tiny face, I was worried she'd throw an equally tiny left hook to that woman's jaw.

But it took until she was kicked out of Brownies for me to investigate whether or not there was a connection between my daughter's difficult behavior and her brain. While she wasn't a model Brownie, Emma loved her weekly meetings at a nearby church parish hall—like most of her peers, she grew up in a world of playdates and rarely saw large groups of her friends. Brownie meetings were a chance to be out of school and in the know. She wouldn't have missed that chance voluntarily. What else could be going on?

I disliked my Texas psychiatrist, whose bookshelves contained volumes with titles like *Christian Psychiatry* and *Counseling Through Jesus*, but I did like my therapist. I liked her so much that I wondered why she would ever choose to live in central Texas, reminding my-self again and again that it was none of my business. I mustered up my courage to ask her about Emma; I was terrified to think my child wasn't okay, scared to consider that I might have damaged her, worried that there would be no way to fix her.

She seemed relieved I'd asked her something she could answer. "She might have attention deficit problems," said my therapist. "If you take her to her pediatrician, they have a special test. You an-swer one half of it and give the other half to her teacher; then the doctor evaluates both and decides what to do next."

A two-part test—it sounded almost as comforting as the steps for earning a Girl Scout badge. I asked for the Vanderbilt Assess-ment Scale sheets and gave one to Emma's third-grade teacher, then filled one out at home. If this had been a merit badge, she'd have aced it. "Runs or climbs at inappropriate times," "avoids or dislikes doing things that take effort of concentration," "fidgets and squirms a lot," "doesn't listen" . . .

The list of signs seemed to go on and on, and each item on it was relevant to my lively, bright daughter. Would she be marked for life?

Emma's pediatrician confirmed my suspicions. "She's definitely ADHD," he told us. "No wonder she's been having such a tough time in school and with activities. I recommend that we get her started on a dose of Adderall. She'll need to take one pill at home in the morning and another midday at school from the nurse."

When that pediatrician told me there was medication to help Emma, I was happy, but I also had plenty of opposition. Long be-fore our war on vaccinations, there were self-righteous suburban (and urban) moms ready to pounce if you revealed you were put-ting your child on stimulants to treat attention disorders. Their reasons ranged from rational—"You have no idea how those will affect her later in life"—to preachy: "Rather than medicate your child, why not try disciplining her?" My closest friend, whose son was a year or so younger, told me I had a "devil child" but also that "using pills" was wrong. Recently she confessed that her son had terrible ADHD and would have benefited from childhood treatment and medication.

None of us has the right answer.

For us, the answer seemed to be Adderall. We could see, immediately, that it helped Emma calm down and take time to make choices instead of acting impulsively.

But this was 2001. Extended-release stimulants for children hadn't come on the market yet, so Emma had to leave her classroom each day in the middle of a regular lesson to head to the school nurse's office for her next dose. She hated it. She hated having to leave when something was going on, and she hated the questions her classmates asked.

She had to go—otherwise the nurse would have called, I would have checked, the doctor would have questioned why she wasn't getting refills—but she hated it. She felt she was different, set apart in a bad way. Marked for life.

———

Emma didn't become compliant with her meds until college; the school years before that were challenging times for everyone. I'd resisted taking my own meds for years, worried that ingesting amphetamines was akin to taking street drugs, the kind that made college friends zip through exam weeks.

All of us made a lot of mistakes, and I felt my daughter's missteps as my own. She is, after all, part of my heart. That's not just sentimental talk. We know that women who have carried children to term retain those children's cells in their own bodies. My daughter lives in me as much as my DNA lives in her.

I also feel that I've made many missteps in seeking treatment

for her attention disorder, missteps in following through on rec-
ommendations, missteps in helping her manage her own disorders,
because that's what attention problems are, disorders, not diseases
or disabilities. (Does that even matter?) I feel this keenly because I
believe that I am my daughter's fiercest advocate.

With the help of Emma's child psychiatrist, I pursued a 504 cer-
tificate for her, a school formality that would allow Emma special
dispensations for her ADHD, including the option to take tests in a
quiet room and extra time to turn in assignments.

It took a great deal of time and trouble to get the 504, which
is many steps simpler to obtain than an Individualized Education
Plan, or IEP. I was the parent who went after it, personally realizing
how essential it is to get some kind of support in place for attention
disorders.

Putting the 504 in place required several meetings with about
a dozen middle school and county education people: special-
education administrators, the school psychologist, a principal
or two, and so on. At one such meeting, with Emma also in the
room, the middle school psychologist took issue with the diagnosis
of ADHD with depression Emma's psychologist had sent in, a diagnosis that I saw in action every day at home.

The psychologist folded her hands and said, "I don't believe
Emma has these problems. I believe her issues are emotional and
need to be addressed in the family." She sat back, lips pursed, gaz-
ing at me.

That gaze might as well have been a red flag. I know I did not
snort or paw the ground, but I took a deep cleansing breath and
responded.

"Ms. X, I am sure your qualifications as a school psychologist
are sound, but I am also sure that they do not qualify you as a medical doctor, which is what my daughter's psychiatrist most surely
is. You may believe that Emma has emotional problems *as well as*

ADHD and depression, but I will not allow you to countermand a doctor's diagnosis in a meeting as if it were made by me with my finger in a copy of a family-health guide. Emma has an official diagnosis of ADHD, and she *will* receive all the support due to her as a student in this county's schools."

Needless to say, Emma's 504 was granted.

Much more important was the look on Emma's face as she listened to me arguing on her behalf. For years I'd been supporting her, but she'd never witnessed it, never heard it. I saw her eyebrows go up to her hairline as she realized her mother fought for her.

When we got home, she leaned against my left shoulder and put her head to my cheek. "Thank you, Mom," she said.

9

—

THE DISAPPEARING WIFE

SINCE OUR 1985 WEDDING DAY, I HAVE GAINED EIGHTY pounds. To be honest, I think at one point I was actually double my wedding-day weight.

It is not easy for me to write that, even if it's factual—and obvious. I know it's obvious because I have heard various comments over the decades from friends and family members about my weight, how it affects my appearance, what it's doing to my health. I'm not the first person to say this: those of us who are overweight know it. We don't necessarily love it either.

But while I dislike acknowledging my weight gain, I also know it's more than a matter of accumulated substance. It is the weight of frustration, disappointment, sadness, grief, and depression. The first half of it crept up, year by year, as I drowned my sorrows with food and drink, not paying attention to my consumption because I thought no one was paying attention to me. The second half of it arrived like a bomb after my father's death. The Germans have a word for it: *Kümmerspeck*. Grief bacon. Being enveloped by fat in response to loss. The French have a word for it too: one is *enrobée*, literally wearing a dress made of fat.

Because, as we overweight people know, while accumulated

fat can be triggered by many things, from trauma to hormones to overeating, we live inside it. Our essential selves are surrounded by fat, and, whatever your reaction to that fat may be, we're still there. Inside. Longing to be seen.

My weight gain has less to do with consumption and more to do with inactivity. It has everything to do with inactivity.

JUST AFTER ADAM and I got married, I read a short story in which a retired British general officer's wife mysteriously loses the ability to walk and must be carried everywhere. She's achieved total passivity in the context of their relationship, which of course reflects the total passivity demanded of her by military life. When I read it, it shocked me, but I still didn't manage to heed its warning. I was a new kind of military spouse, I believed, not of that character's generation or inclination. I was going to keep my own name, forge my own path, have my own career.

Every time something frightened me—work, moving, academia, new parenthood, moving, teaching, miscarriage, moving, and so on—I stopped moving. Instead of fight or flight, I, like a rabbit, opted for freeze. While we lived in Berlin, I ran four miles a day, but as we started our move back to the United States, I stopped running. The pounds piled on. I tried running while we were in graduate school, but the work so overwhelmed me I couldn't cope with fitting exercise into my schedule. I walked while I was pregnant with Emma, but once we landed in central Texas the landscape depressed me too much to do more than push her carriage around the block once a day. I didn't gain a lot during my pregnancies. I just didn't lose the pounds that piled on between them.

With every bit of bulk, I could feel myself disappearing. I was less noticeable. Less troublesome. Less interesting. Less appealing. Less threatening. Just a soft, then plump, then chubby, then heavy, then obese woman. I no longer mattered as an attractive woman, or a woman to envy, or even as a person who could generate confidence and authority. I was a fat wife, a fat mom, a fat friend, a fat daughter, a fat sister, a fat colleague, defined by fat instead of by dreams or desires or anger.

Any kind of movement, even the simplest bit of housework, felt like too much. I should have noticed this, should have understood this was depression. I just thought it was the way I was made. I was right. It was my genetic inheritance combined with the severe stress of marriage into the military. Even after I'd acknowledged and been treated for depression, movement seemed impossible. I was taking antidepressants, I was going to therapy—what more could I do? I never wanted to move, to leave a chair or a sofa. The idea of being interested in a walk was completely beyond me. Who were these people who looked forward to aerobics classes?

Every time I put forth a tendril toward exercise, someone pushed me too far—or I saw them pushing themselves too far and balked. It wasn't enough to run a mile or two with my friend Maggie when we were in Berlin; she wanted me to run three miles, then five. I walked with a fellow graduate student in Charlottesville who not only insisted that we go every day, despite a punishing schedule, but who grew increasingly orthorexic (orthorexia is an obsession with right eating) in an attempt to shed her own weight, at one point consuming mainly baked chicken thighs and coffee with skim milk. My college friend Hanna moved without ceasing, a coping mechanism for her severe anxiety, scolding me when I sat still for too long during visits. She would encourage me to join her for a short walk that always turned into several miles and that left me, the unexercised one, short of breath, sweaty, and angry. When we met Frances, she was going through a divorce and was determined to become a yummy mummy. She would ask me and Adam to accompany her on a run; then she'd sprint ahead with Adam, leaving me sweaty and angry again while they laughed at my slow pace.

There was something wrong with me, with my weight and attitude toward exercise, and I didn't know what it was. All I knew was that I was too slow and too sedentary and too big. But the more friends and family poked at me through the bars of my fat cage, the angrier I got. Why couldn't they leave me alone? What did my weight and sloth have to do with them? I wanted to disappear, to live somewhere beyond their prying eyes and comments, somewhere I wasn't expected to be a fit officer's wife who wore leggings to pick up the kids from school, where I wasn't expected to spend my precious alone time racking up miles on a treadmill, where I wasn't constantly thinking about the calorie content of every bite I placed in my mouth.

Maybe if I disappeared I wouldn't have to think about what it meant for Adam to have an angry, depressed, increasingly heavy wife.

———

"Army Wife: Toughest Job in the Army" read the apron I received for Christmas just days before Adam and I took our vows at the West Point Cadet Chapel. So many laughs, because even though the aphorism is true, it's not supposed to be acknowledged. Everyone knows the soldier has the toughest job; the soldier is putting his life on the line, and the wife gets to stay home and share in the bounty of his paycheck and benefits while he works a twelve-hour day that starts with tough exercise.

Adam's job will always be the most important, the one that supported our family, the one that still supports me now that our daughters are adults with their own jobs and health insurance. Adam's job carries the health insurance that allows me to receive my medications for a very reasonable cost, that gives me the freedom to work as a writer, because while I have a career, I don't make a living. Why wouldn't I want to disappear?

The work I can accomplish without threatening my mental stability has little value in the free-market economy. That's true for most writers I know. The difference, for me, is that the work I can accomplish without threatening my mental stability has little value for my husband.

Adam and I made some assumptions about each other early on that continue to affect our marriage and relationship. He assumed that since I wanted to work, I wanted to have a career similar to his own: steady, government-based, with regular opportunities for promotion. I assumed that, since his father and most of their family friends had been permanent professors at West Point, and since Adam had achieved a great deal academically, at some point he would leave active duty and get a doctoral degree and then a tenured position at a college or university.

Army wives, now more accurately known as military spouses, who relish their role do exist. I know many of them who prefer not to work outside the home and whose contributions to on-post volunteer organizations allow a great deal of good to be done. To me, it's like being an avid gardener—or not. You can't force yourself to love digging in the dirt and planting. You can't force yourself to love pruning and weeding. But for some people it comes very naturally.

I knew I wanted something different, but how could I ask for what I wanted when I hadn't even given myself time to find out what that was? I arrived at midlife, married with children, having dabbled in editing, teaching, and writing, but with few strong skills in any of those fields—including child rearing. The more weight I put on, the more distant I felt from any kind of achievement and fulfillment.

The more weight I put on, the more distant I felt from any choice other than the ones I had already made.

When we were in college, Adam chose to be posted in West Berlin rather than Colorado—where I had a job. When it was time to go to graduate school, we went to the University of Virginia because that was the best place for Adam. When we went to Texas, it was for Adam's new job. When we finally got back to Virginia, we left early because Adam was selected for a military school. It was a pattern.

Eleven moves in twenty-one years. Seven to ten pounds for each move, weight that sometimes came off, only to return during the next move. And through every relocation I moved less, except for a brief couple of years in Texas when, once both girls were finally in school for the day, I would force myself out the door and walk myself into a trance on a four-mile loop through our strange neighborhood bordered by a golf course, where no one was ever outside their houses, no matter the weather. Texans learn to stay indoors in the searing heat and enjoy the outdoors in their backyards, often sheltered by live oaks—their front yards are merely to show off well-watered lawns.

I did lose weight those two years, but when it was time to move again I gained it all back. Any disruption in routine derailed my commitment to regular exercise. Any disruption in routine derailed, for that matter, my commitment to my treatment and medications. I might run out of meds, or forget to schedule an appointment with a new doctor, or stop taking my antidepressants because I thought my libido would return.

When Adam moved from one job to the next, there was a paper trail and people for him to talk to about how to integrate into the office. But where were my peers? The women with whom I'd gone to college, the people I'd studied with in graduate school—they were pursuing their own paths. The fellow military spouses around me in these various locations often didn't have paths of their own that I wanted to follow. They planned potlucks, volunteered at the

military hospitals, almost always the maternity ward, and organized family-fun days to support unit cohesion.

They also seemed to do one of two things: kept their girlish figures or let them go entirely. I struggled not to put on more pounds
even as I did so, but found two species around me, Lycra-clad ga-
zelles who spent their mornings at the gym or doughy matrons in
smocks who spent their mornings baking. Where were the others,
the in-betweens, the spouses who would rather organize a protest
or spend the weekend reading a thick book than attend one more
baby shower for a mere acquaintance?

Those women did not exist fifteen to twenty years ago. I now
know a tiny cadre of other milspouses who are writers, and each of
us has experienced the loneliness I knew, even the ones who did a
much better job of fitting in than I ever did.

———

Every single pound I've gained in the last thirty-five years equals an
idea I didn't pursue, pages I didn't write, hours I didn't give to my
creative work and therefore resented with my whole heart.

That doesn't mean I wish I weren't married. I love Adam more
now than I did decades ago. I fell in love with a person, not a military career. It doesn't mean I wish I weren't a mother. I love our
daughters more now than I did on the days they were born. In spite
of how I've failed them, I'd never choose remaining childfree.

What I do wish is that I'd held on to my writer self that I'd begun to nurture in college. I knew long before that I wanted to be a
writer, although I didn't really know any writers, didn't understand
the kinds of careers writers could have or how a person developed
a creative career.

My parents said, "Writing isn't a career. You should study com-
puter science. That's the future."

My teachers said, "We don't know many writers, but you'll be a terrific English instructor."

My friends said, "We're not sure what you're up to. We're studying accounting/engineering/nursing/computer science."

But once I was in college, I met people who were writers, people who wanted to be writers, libraries that were filled with the output of writers and academics and journalists. There was the housemate who papered her wastebasket with rejection slips from *The New Yorker*, the classmate who edited the literary magazine, the friends with parents who were authors and painters and publishers. It took a while, but by the spring of my sophomore year I began to unfurl the tiniest bit.

I had to stop myself from a life of errors. Marrying into the military was, depression told me, a surefire way to make errors stop.

Depression was wrong, of course. I had so many new errors to make as a military spouse, and I made most of them.

The one mistake I had not made was to marry a person I loved with all my heart, and still do. Adam and I have not had a perfect marriage. Thank goodness. What bores we would be. Between my mistakes and his, combined with circumstance, we've had our ups and downs. I don't know how I managed to choose a life partner correctly when I kept myself from being who I truly wanted to be for so long.

It may not surprise you to learn that Adam has also gained weight since our wedding day. The weight of depression takes its toll on the caregiver too. And while his weight came on more suddenly, in the years since his retirement from active duty, it did come. Depression and caregiving have taken a toll on our bodies and our health and our appearances.

The good news, quickly: We're both doing much better. We take care of our health, and we've lost weight, become more fit, and are working toward more progress.

The bad news, more slowly: The fear and anxiety that made up my depression weren't all from outside stress, much as I found it convenient to blame the military life I didn't enjoy. Much of it came from within me, from brain chemistry, heredity, and childhood trauma. While it would have helped to have received a proper diagnosis of double depression much sooner, I would still have had to work through layers of pain and poor health and bad communication in order to be healthy.

Adam would still have been there, whether I worked through those layers earlier or later. I do not want to canonize him. Like me, he has made plenty of mistakes.

The weight we both carry has a lot to do with the stops and starts of our understanding about each other's needs. We communicate very well; more than one therapist has noted that our ability to state things to each other clearly and without recrimination is remarkable.

But we come from wildly different places, and for such a long time we were both attempting to make me fit into his mold. I made the mold's bad fit worse by getting bigger and bigger. You can whittle down my persona, I seemed to say, but you'll never make me small. I will not fit in. I will not fit. I will not.

The crucial thing is that while I felt I had to at least make attempts, however feeble, to fit into Adam's world, the reverse was never true—because his job was always paramount. Our daughters tell me I made a choice and I should have known what that choice entailed. I should have understood what the military was all about.

Easy for them to say, as so-called military brats. Not only did they grow up knowing the words *commissary* and *quarters*; they both went to middle school and high school here in northern Virginia, where active duty and retired military families are as common as azalea bushes. Everyone around them understands the contract, they think.

I didn't. Perhaps I would have paid more attention, been clued in, if I hadn't been simultaneously coping with a new lifestyle and an old illness. From the moment I decided I wanted to spend my entire life with Adam, I've been part of a system carefully calibrated to privilege soldiers over spouses. I won't even argue that it should be any other way. But I will argue if you tell me I should have understood, should have known—what did I expect? I didn't. I got it wrong. Maybe I should have been sensible and walked away, leaving Adam to his path and me to mine. Maybe I should have been pragmatic and submitted, realizing that a couple of decades were nothing in the grand scheme of things.

I got it wrong. I struggled. I thrashed. I hated. Those responses contributed to my depression. But they did not cause my depression, especially not its double nature. If I'd known I had double depression, would I still have gotten married? Maybe—because I would, then, have been on medications that made things clearer to me. But maybe that clarity would have meant that I walked away. Maybe I would have been able to see that what I really wanted to do was pursue a life as a writer, for better or worse.

———

Thirty-five years later, I can tell you we're on the same page. Was that worth eighty pounds? Twelve moves? The major depressive episodes? The toll taken on Adam as caregiver, on our children as minors, on my writing?

It's so easy, now, to say yes. We are happy, healthy, getting fit, privileged by income and location and education and belongings. It's so easy to claim it was all worth it. In a way, it was, in that same way everyone's life is.

But sometimes I like to imagine an Adam and a Bethanne who broke up, endured some heartbreak, and then moved on to different lives. Not because I am trying to erase this life but because I want to acknowledge the man who didn't disappear into caregiving and the woman who didn't disappear into an ill-fitting role. I want to remember that we both made choices. That the ones we make now we see much more clearly and therefore hold more dearly.

10

MOVING BOXES

A FEW YEARS AGO, OUR GARAGE SPRUNG A LEAK. What does that mean? I have no idea; what I do know is that after the leak had been diagnosed by a plumber, our insurance company sent out a team of people to pack up everything in the garage, trash and treasure, no distinctions, sheer efficiency. All the resulting boxes were placed in a temporary pod that sat at the bottom of our driveway.

Another team of people came in the following week to repair the leak, then scrape, paint, and clean the garage. If you've never seen a completely empty, spanking-clean two-car garage, well, it's a thing of beauty. After another team emptied the pod and put all the boxes back in place, it was still a thing of beauty, smelling of fresh paint and clean cardboard from the moving boxes.

It didn't stay that way. We are not always the most organized family—by *we* I mean Adam, who seems to almost delight in keeping cords and hoses uncoiled and the lawn mower covered in grass cuttings, in piling unwanted objects into half-full containers. Even the global pandemic of 2020 didn't inspire household-management action. We always found something else to do. We walked a lot of local trails and caught up on a lot of old movies while we maintained social distance.

However, I'd been in this situation before, and I knew I could tackle the job again, so in 2021 I started spending an hour each weekend opening some of these boxes and donating, resituating, or sometimes trashing their contents. The team who packed them hadn't taken much care; mildewed items crammed in with other things meant a stash of old shoes had to be thrown away, for example. Many boxes held just one strange or bulky thing, like a wreath for the front door or a car-trunk organizer. So much cardboard for so little good. I tried to remember to remain thankful for the people who had made a dry garage possible, and to hope that one day it would once again be a place to park two cars instead of being a repository for bags of books and a rack of clothes too nice to part with but too seldom worn.

I sometimes wonder what the tally would be if we'd kept track of all the moving boxes filled with our household goods over our combined eleven moves. There may be a record of those that were handled by the military, but we did a lot of our own hauling to keep costs down for the final two moves, so it would be hard to arrive at a number. It's the sheer volume of boxes that interests me rather than the actual number. We've taken up so much space over the years.

Depression has taken up so much space in me over the years. Relocating from one place to another, whether across the ocean, the country, or the same town, holds a great deal of stress. Add that stress to the headspace of a person already afflicted with depression and you have a recipe for a breakdown. Or, in my case, many breakdowns. At least eleven of them.

Moving has never become easier for me, and neither has depression. Before menopause, I never, ever came to terms with my monthly period. Even though I knew when it was due, even when I was cranky and bloated, its arrival would surprise me. Depressive episodes startle me, even when I think back and realize I've done too much or had a heartache.

For several of our moves, I had women in my life to "help." People who always mean well. All of us do when we decide to help. But some people actually lift you up and make things easier, better, and more fun, while others judge and impose.

Exactly like the friends, family, and colleagues who see or feel or hear about my depression. Some, who have experienced mood disorders, will empathize. Some who have not can't even sympathize. The vast majority remain confused as to what I'm experiencing, and why shouldn't they? For most of the years we were moving from one place to another, I was confused. I took my antidepressant medication. I dutifully found a therapist and a psychiatrist in each place we lived. Until our penultimate move, when things got much worse, I kept up an exercise routine, propelling myself out for walks and swims and runs because everyone told me exercise and fresh air would make me feel better. Exercise has never changed my mood, ever, and I don't think it ever will, although it often tames my anxieties, now that I can distinguish between depression and anxiety.

It's an important distinction. Until 2016, when I experienced life without any depression for the first time, I thought anxiety manifested as hand-wringing, classic worry behavior. I often thought, on being around someone with severe anxiety, *At least I don't feel like that! At least I can just go to sleep when I'm upset.* I was as ignorant of how anxiety manifests as those others were about how depression manifests.

Now I see that every day was like opening boxes the contents of which I didn't know. Would today be a day when the box contained depression and I wouldn't be able to get out of or stay away from my bed? Or would today's box hold anxiety, heralding hours spent worrying and stressing out about the simplest interaction I'd had with a colleague or friend? Maybe it would be a box of both (even though I didn't understand that, not then) and I'd lie in bed fretting about my poor performance on a project or how to respond to an upsetting message from my sister.

When you remain in a lifestyle that doesn't work for you, that you dislike, that doesn't feed your dreams, it's inevitable that you find yourself out of sorts. That doesn't mean you have a mental illness. It might mean you live in a restrictive culture or that you made a bad decision; it might mean that you, like me, fell head over heels in love and didn't think about the consequences.

So you put this bad experience in a mental box, tape it shut. Then another one. Sometimes you put good experiences, whole swathes of time, in mental boxes, because they're over and you don't have them and you have to confront what's right in front of you, a new house and new friends and new activities.

––––

There is a medieval concept called the memory palace, in which you create a huge and never-ending structure in your mind where different rooms hold different kinds of knowledge. The concept was particularly appealing and helpful, I imagine, during a time when humans were beginning to amass large amounts of data (their data being less mathematic and more lexicographic). You might have a room for scriptural passages, one for poems, one for taxonomies, and so forth. A memory palace is meant to be quite spacious, organized, and easy to navigate. Like a real palace, there should be clear signage and proper shelving. (It's also one of the reasons why the British critic Tony Judt ironically named his memoir *The Memory Chalet*; suffering as Judt was from amyotrophic lateral sclerosis, he knew that his recollections might need to be crammed into a smaller space during a shorter period of time.)

By the time we'd muddled through our thirties and the six moves we negotiated in that decade, Adam and I were mentally and emotionally exhausted. We had two growing children whose care displaced many other aspects of life, from organizational to social to professional. Our respective memory palaces were swollen with information about Emma's severe asthma, Martha's displaced incisors, early-model cell phones that needed charging, shopping lists, and forgotten deadlines (mostly mine).

I couldn't cope. And then Adam decided that I should look for a job.

That's unfair. What really happened was that Adam saw my frustration at never having been able to establish a career given our constant moving. He decided that we wouldn't move again, that after his next promotion (to lieutenant colonel) came through, he would finish that assignment and retire from active duty.

All so our children could experience some stability and I could find stable work.

If we'd realized I was still ill and not properly treated, would either of us have tried so hard for me to pursue a career?

If I understood more about what it takes to be a writer, would I have pushed so hard to find a full-time job?

I'd tried various paths and believed I failed at all of them. Pursuing a PhD—dead end. Teaching community college—failed there too. Writing PR and communications content—wasn't sure how to follow through and get more gigs. Pitching and writing freelance lifestyle articles—same problem, plus the dream publications made you jump through an ever-increasing number of hoops.

Adam thought I'd be happiest with a government job akin to his own. He was projecting, but not out of controlling motives. He heard me bewail my fate and knew that I was frustrated by not being able to make regular money or gain any kind of professional status. He was listening. He cared about me. He wanted me to go after something that would solve my problems and, so he thought, make me happy.

Unfortunately, he was listening to a woefully unreliable narrator, a person who thought she needed one kind of path when she was actually made for another. The moving boxes in my head that weren't devoted to practical family matters were filled with knowledge about literature, books, and authors. I had very little interest in unpacking those related to anything else; my undergraduate political science courses remain in a dusty mental storage room, as do those from working as an editor of government regulations and the little I learned while writing middle school social studies curricula.

The boxes filled with bookish knowledge had been temporarily displaced by boxes filled with ideas about what a real career looked like. In the late 1990s and early 2000s, no one I knew was telecommuting. The men I knew, who were mostly military officers, went to work at their units and were usually away from home for twelve or more hours at a time. The women I knew were divided between stay-at-home mothers and career women.

We were put into boxes. Stay-at-home moms (SAHMs) had schedules almost more rigid than the working women. A friend who was considered a milspouse leader began her day with a workout while her kids were still asleep, cooked her husband breakfast while he was home showering after his physical training, then swept and mopped the floors after making her children's school lunches. Once the kids were in their classrooms, she did her grocery shopping at the commissary and listened to a book on tape while she ate a salad for lunch and then tidied up the bedrooms. Afternoons were for family correspondence and organizing before picking up the kids and taking them to various after-school activities, snacks in a cooler in the backseat. Back home there was dinner to prepare, homework to supervise, then baths, bedtime, laundry, an hour of TV with the husband if he wasn't away on an exercise.

This is a true account of one woman I knew; she was motivated and energetic, but she wasn't the only one who kept up such a dynamic daily routine. It mostly felt as if I were the only one who didn't.

A working friend's day sounded slightly more frantic but also included more adult time: She ran at 5:00 a.m., took care of the kids' clothing and school run while her husband left for his nearby legal office, then did some work or read a book on the train into Manhattan. A director of human resources for a tech company, she started her day with several meetings, often lunched with a boss or a mentee, got through paperwork in the afternoon, and met the same train each evening to be home for a family meal and then ferrying the kids to activities (her husband did the afternoon school pickup). She always had more work to do at night, as I heard about during our occasional phone calls. The housecleaning was taken care of by Merry Maids, who descended once a week with buckets and bottles and brooms.

To me, enmeshed in my ideas of what mattered and what made a person matter, this second friend's day sounded far superior to the SAHM's day. There were demarcations and shared household labor and a defined place at the corporate table. These were the things I'd grown up to value.

I lived among SAHMs. I was educated among career women. I was married to a man brought up to ace tests, win awards, and earn medals. But I still hadn't figured out who I was.

My days varied wildly, according to how low my mood was. Sometimes it was just low energy, sometimes it was sadness, sometimes it was despair. On my best days, I would awake without effort, manage to get clean and dressed, and leave the house on time to bring our daughters to school and make it to whichever job I was in and/or back to my desk at an appropriate hour. On those best days—which seemed to occur less and less as the years went by—I would check tasks and meetings off my list, enjoy a social lunch hour, maybe even have time for a gossipy afternoon coffee break or a brisk walk before leaving on time (like the career parents I knew) to pick up the kids.

On my worst days, I'd wrench myself out of bed, manage the bare minimum of hygiene and style, and get the kids to school in a fog of self-loathing and fatigue that must have made me seem to them like a beast, some kind of cartoon creature with coffee in one hand and car keys in the other. I'd sit at a desk, stare, and distract myself with whatever version of web surfing was available, depending on the year. I started with heavy eBay scrolling (although not necessarily purchasing), moved on to listserves (the long-defunct Readerville was a favorite), and then to Facebook the minute it opened to colleges outside of Harvard. I thought I was very good at concealing my inability to work, but I probably wasn't. I was probably about as good at hiding my web surfing as I was at pretending to be cheerful in front of my immediate family.

However, the worst thing about any of my days was the way I felt. Inside I teemed with worms of self-loathing and recrimination. If I managed to get a few things done properly, I could not smile and think, *Great job!* I might as well have been walking on knives and wearing a hat secured to my head by nails. The pain of existing, of knowing that I had to keep moving through a world that made me miserable, was excruciating.

My only defense was to pack more things into boxes, to say to myself, Yes, you're awfully unattractive, but let's think about that later. Yes, you're heading into menopause and nothing works right anymore, but let's think about that later. Yes, you screw up your daughters every day, but let's think about that later. Yes, you hate this company and you'd like to be somewhere else, but let's think about that later. I was always trying to get on to the next thing, because whatever I was doing was so hard. I mean every single thing was so hard. I didn't want to be typing, or talking on the phone, or standing in line to pay for new socks, or attending an elementary school soccer match. I also didn't want to be eating a nice dinner, or watching television to relax, or taking a walk in the sunshine.

Everything made me miserable. I threw it all in boxes and put it away and just kept existing because what else could I do if I wasn't brave enough to die? My essential self, I decided, must be weak and rotting if I couldn't even muster up enough enthusiasm to go to a party or answer an email in a timely manner. After all, I was medicated. I went to therapy. I couldn't be depressed, because I was being treated for depression, and if I was still depressed while being treated for depression, that meant I was soft. Lazy. Definitely not of staunch character.

From time to time as I opened the remaining boxes in our garage, I discovered something delightful that I forgot we owned. An heirloom lace tablecloth that was supposed to go out for dry-cleaning (and that now, years later, has been cleaned and properly stored). A letter from summer camp written by Martha, asking for more *magazeens*. A favorite sweater.

Similarly, from time to time as I lived under a depressive cloud, I would experience a moment or an hour or a day (rarely longer) of contentment. The New Year's Eve when, still stuck in Texas, we decided to have a family dance party, and the joy this brought to our two wriggly girls thawed my soul long enough to join in and laugh for several hours. Days at the beach on Cape Cod when we knew we could stay late and have hot dogs and ice cream cones for dinner. Occasional short trips away for our wedding anniversary if my parents were available to babysit. I knew what happiness felt like, but I experienced it so seldom, and that made me believe that everything had to be perfect in order for happiness to happen, or that happiness only occurred under the most balanced circumstances.

The truth was that I had to be perfectly balanced to experience the happiness, not the reverse. I lived with depression, even though

I thought I was permanently flawed, and the moments of happiness had to be pretty amazing to break through the fog that existed between the world and me.

No wonder I needed The Best of whatever it was I needed: it took something that was superb in every detail to make an impression on me. When bad things happened during a holiday or celebration, they weren't just bad things—I had caused them. I'm not sure if I'm qualified to diagnose whatever personality problem this is, but I know it went hand in hand with being depressed. Only superlatives—the best, the happiest, the funniest, the most x or y—brought any pleasure.

I've never been catatonic. I hope I never am. But I still felt somehow encased, entrapped, in a shell. I couldn't break through that shell to communicate with my husband or our daughters. And it wasn't just about joy. I couldn't break through that shell to say no to anyone either. No, I will not take on this extra work. No, I cannot solve your problems. No, I am not available to talk on the phone right now. No, that is too much to ask of me.

Which is where the moving boxes metaphor ends. Boxes have good boundaries. I did not. Put something in a box, tape it closed, and it won't be used, or misused. For all my attempts to keep things contained, I was a human with an undiagnosed mental illness, a person whose boundaries were regularly violated, mostly by other people who meant no harm but had no idea they were interacting with an ill person.

11

COMING UNBOUND

IN 2001, I GOT A LUCKY BREAK. I MET A MAGAZINE editor at a conference and convinced him to let me telecommute; that magazine was called *PAGES*, and it was all about books and authors.

PAGES would run for only five years. Its end came about dramatically, when the publisher and managing editor were discovered to have fraudulently spiked subscription numbers, and the Securities and Exchange Commission raided their offices. Fortunately, the editorial side had nothing to do with any of that, and by the time it happened I'd moved on to a new job anyway.

The important thing about my work there is that it shifted me from a very low point, stuck in central Texas for the second time with two young children and a husband who was working long post-9/11 hours, onto a track where I was regularly interviewing authors and communicating with the media. I was then, and now, incredibly high functioning. I was able to finish two degrees, sustain a marriage, get hired for various jobs, and raise two children, as well as do things like buy appropriate clothing, send out holiday cards, plan vacations, and (sometimes) remember friends' birthdays.

But high functioning does not equal healthy. Unbeknownst to me, I didn't even know what being healthy felt like, let alone how to maintain it.

Because I'd been moving around so much, pulling up roots that hadn't had time to develop, I didn't learn much about how to collaborate and work with teams, especially in a professional environment. The army will tell you again and again that volunteer opportunities for spouses can provide great experience for future jobs and careers; unfortunately, I was so turned off by everything military that I wanted nothing to do with spouse groups or on-post institutions.

So there I was, in my late thirties, when I was hired as the books editor at AOL—though I had almost no experience working with other people. When I did work with others, my low moods, low energy, and defensive crouch made communication difficult, if not impossible. I made plenty of demands but didn't deliver on tasks assigned to me. I considered deadlines as elastic as a wad of bubble gum. I allowed my excitement about my own position's developments to override meeting decorum, fretted every time my manager didn't recognize those developments, and wasted a lot of time walking around and chatting with whichever colleagues wouldn't shoo me away from their cubicles.

To be fair, sometimes other people's dysfunction met up with mine and caused problems. Hired as a book publicist at an august organization, I found myself walked to an office and left there, not so much as a "Here's the ladies' room" from my new boss. For the first time, I began having severe panic attacks, the kind where you shake and everything goes blurry and you want to vomit.

I quit that job to host an author-interview series for our local PBS affiliate, which would run for over three years and offer even more opportunities to meet people in the media world. The show was filmed like a real television production, in the same studio where Gwen Ifill hosted *Washington Week*. I had hair and makeup, a producer, a camera crew, a talent booker. It all went quickly to my head, in the sense that I forgot the show wasn't everyone's top priority. I overbooked guests, assumed my producer could drop what he was doing at a moment's notice, and generally pissed off my colleagues.

My next position was as a telecommuting newsletter editor. I had to wake at 5:00 a.m. every day to be ready to read as much trade news about books and publishing as possible before deciding what I needed to write or assign or drop into a template. My editor and I got along terrifically well; I never missed a deadline and I never slept through my hideously early alarm. Unfortunately, my complete inability to file invoices and reimbursements on time held everybody up, so I was dismissed.

At this point, I still believed that, despite my errors and occasional bad luck, I had something to contribute to the world of journalism. When two young men I knew only through an acquaintance approached me about heading up their new website as CEO, I demurred and asked to be called executive editor instead. I expected that I would be brought on board with an official meeting and be shown the site and that then we would start building its content together.

Instead, less than a week after I'd signed a bunch of paperwork (including vesting as the CEO, with stock options), I awoke to find Twitter on fire with a famous author blasting me for my poor editorial decisions. I hadn't realized the site was already publishing content. Being fired from that job threw me into a very deep abyss, the one that forced me into a psychiatric hospital. Being fired is never easy, but it's especially hard when you take everything personally and are prone to chemical depression. Now I know that, without completely different caregivers and treatment, I could have used that firing to examine my behavior, to change it, let alone recognize the event as something that was handled poorly by my bosses.

I WAS SOMEONE who failed up several times. I wondered if I had lost all chance of working in my beloved chosen field.

I disappeared behind a wall of shame, both personally and professionally. I was trying to raise two strong feminist daughters, even though I wasn't yet able to see how poorly I was doing in that respect, and I couldn't even show them a mother who was a great professional. I couldn't make enough money to make a difference in our household budget. The small amounts I brought in offset a shopping spree or three but didn't allow us to, say, take a fantastic family vacation or buy a new car.

The more you agree with a painful comment or observation, the closer shame snuggles in, and the greater the amount of shame you feel. Everything everyone said about me stung, and mostly they weren't saying anything. It was all in my head. If I could have gotten paid for self-recriminations, I'd have had enough for several fantastic vacations.

———

Every rejection at work, be it a meeting someone was too busy to make, a boss pulling me up short for a sloppily prepared presentation, or a mildly snide comment from a colleague, sent me to the same place: depression. It didn't matter if it was my fault or not. I couldn't own up to anything because if I did it might mean I was fatally flawed, and if I was, how could I keep going? Depression told me it would be best if I took my flawed self and hid. Call in sick. Call in sick again. Disappear for weeks after losing a position; stop calling friends and family and sink into the realm of least resistance. If I didn't do anything at all, I couldn't disappoint anyone.

There was one Christmas celebration when I couldn't muster enough energy to wrap any gifts. Several years without holiday cards written or mailed. Events to which we planned to go, but at the last minute I would send regrets, unable to uncurl my body from the fetal position. A Thanksgiving when I had the flu and there was no table set, no dinner made, no gratitude expressed. Soccer match after soccer match unattended. Packages mailed years after their intended recipients should have received them.

With each job loss I felt diminished. I had somehow internalized the idea that I was my job. I no longer want to place blame on anyone but myself for this idea, but I do see where I went wrong. I thought my mother only cared about my achievements, but what she actually cared about was my future happiness and stability. I thought Adam only cared about my bringing in money, but he was focused on helping me find something that would make me feel secure. I thought our daughters needed a working mother, when they actually needed a mom who worked on their behalf.

I thought I needed someone to believe in me, when the one person who needed to believe in me was myself.

12

IN ABSENTIA

O N A WINTER'S DAY, ADAM AND I PLAY HOOKY FROM work and head downtown to the Hirshhorn Museum. There's a Jean Arp exhibit I want to see. I admire the Dadaists because, as I tell Adam, they sought to make meaning after the terrors of World War I rendered much art meaningless.

He disagrees with me, although with great good humor, the cheerful irony he maintains whenever he encounters something he doesn't understand. "These sketches just don't make sense," he laughs. "What kind of drugs did these people take?"

It's not that he mocks or dislikes all art. In fact, as we enter an exhibit on modernism, we go our separate ways for a few minutes, each fascinated by different types of paintings and sculptures. Then we meet as we each cross in front of a cast-bronze figure, an animated expression on its round face, limbs and torso not active in any identifiable activity except mischief.

"It's Emma!" we both exclaim.

Our first child's family nickname is "Hurricane Emma." Whenever and wherever she lights down, she simultaneously takes charge and wreaks havoc. An old friend, meeting four-year-old

Emma, opined that our daughter would either run the world one day or burn it down.

Now I think, Maybe she'll run the world by burning it down, and that might not be such a bad thing.

Emma is a marvel of a young woman who works at one of the largest tech companies in the nation, lives an active and fun life in Colorado, and has many friends. She is beloved, by them and by us.

She also knows that communicating with her can be a challenge. During a holiday last year she mentioned she'd stay with a friend "as long as I don't annoy him."

"Why would you annoy him?" I asked.

She looked at me sideways and cackled. "Because I'm annoying!"

My poor little apple didn't fall far from the tree. Because I have been annoying, too, and was especially annoying during her tween and teen years, when the misery of several major depressive episodes created a distance between us that may never be completely healed.

———

After Emma graduated from college, she began working in Washington, D.C., commuting to her job from our home in McLean, Virginia, where we'd moved the year before after a decade in nearby Arlington.

Occasionally, when she didn't have plans with her friends, she'd ask me to hang out, have lunch, get our nails done. I knew she was reaching out, wanting to forge a relationship different than we'd had during the worst years of my depression. She wanted me to be light and breezy, to show up and laugh and participate in things she liked—eating vegetarian food, shopping for gym clothes, browsing bookshelves or makeup aisles.

We were trying to be happy as a nuclear family; we were not happy as an extended family; we were mostly estranged. My sister had not yet undergone the ECT sessions that would return her to a kind of stability, and I was still experiencing regular bouts of major depression with suicidal ideation. I didn't feel strong enough to communicate with my sister and her bipolar syndrome and border-line personality syndrome and schizoaffective disorder. I was too weak, too fragile, too needy myself.

The first time Emma and I tried to talk about our difficult past, I was so eager to gain her absolution that I plowed in without thinking about how it might feel for her to hear my apologies.

We went to a Japanese restaurant, her choice. It was a wintry Saturday, and the idea of hot green tea and steaming bowls of udon noodles appealed.

"Honey," I said, "I'm so glad to be here with you."

"I am too, Mom," she replied. "Should we get some rolls? Sashimi?"

The server set down pottery cups of tea. I remember being terrified, afraid that if I didn't tell Emma immediately that I now understood my terrible mistakes as a parent, I never would have the courage again.

I grabbed her hands.

"I'm so sorry that we've had so much trouble in the past," I said. "I am so sorry that things I did and said hurt you."

What did I expect? Was I such a narcissist that I believed she'd squeeze my hands and say it was all okay?

She turned her head to the side and began to cry. Emma and I are both prone to tears, but hers just kept coming.

"Let's just go," she choked out. "Let's just leave, now. This isn't going to work." She stood up and gathered her things.

"No, please—please, Emma, let's stay. Please don't leave." I felt desperate, as if this were my last chance to speak with her.

Maybe it was. Today our relationship, while not perfect, is so different, so much better, that I sometimes wonder what would have happened if I'd let her walk out of the restaurant that afternoon. Not because of her, but because of me. If I hadn't persevered and coaxed her through that tough, weepy lunch, would I have given up on our ability to communicate? Would I have shut down and allowed her, once again, to dictate the terms of our relationship?

At different ages, Emma has accused me of not acting properly adult in our relationship, and I'll allow that my depression and its modalities did sometimes keep me from setting limits. However, not only did I have a coparent and spouse in those periods, but I also faced a child whose own mental challenges included severe ADHD, oppositional-defiant disorder (ODD), and depression. Were those problems genetic? Environmental? It's impossible to say for sure. ADHD can cause ODD. ODD can cause depression. And so on. Not to mention improper parent-child bonding, parental neglect, and lack of supervision, all of which might or might not occur with a depressed parent.

———

A depressed mother. Isn't a mother supposed to be the most important person in a child's life? The most important parent in a child's life? The most essential figure in that child's development?

Yes, according to Emma. Yet I had failed as a mother. She wasn't going to let me off easily, and there's some evidence to say she shouldn't. Another conversation we had, this in our family living room, started because I said something about how she's known some of her friends since middle school, that I thought that showed she was a good person. "Yah," she said. "But middle school was really hard for me."

I nodded and waited. Sometimes I do understand not to fill in the silences.

Tears welled in her eyes. "I was so miserable back then. I was so unhappy. I didn't know how to handle myself, and I didn't have a mom to help me."

I didn't recall her maturation in the same way. I remember a child who had been a lively, gifted fifth grader morph after a move from one Arlington house to another into a sixth grader who fought with us to paint her new room pink, then fought with us because we'd painted her new room pink, a child who changed almost overnight.

When Emma began to struggle during middle school—and I may not have known she was disturbed by her body's changes, but I knew she was disturbed—I wanted to throw myself whole-heartedly into her care and development. I wanted to get her help, I wanted to get her to talk, even though I knew I wasn't always acting from a rational place. The disinterested attitude from her school's administration and faculty enraged me. Each time they called me into a meeting to discuss Emma's ADHD plan and prog-ress, I turned into a furious mama bear who would rather destroy the people in front of me who didn't love my daughter as much as I did than listen to them.

But my care for her was not matched by communication. If I could go back in time to the first moment I knew our older daugh-ter was struggling, I would have devoted myself wholeheartedly to her. I would have stopped pursuing work and talked to her without worrying about the ticking of the clock, the day's deadlines and phone calls and information to be ingested.

I couldn't do that. My husband, my partner, my coparent, didn't want me to give up paying work so I could make things right for our child.

No, it's not that simple. Emma was born when we'd been mar-ried for seven years. We were twenty-nine years old, and while we felt quite youthful, a neighbor who had had her first child at age eighteen reminded me that I wasn't exactly a young mother.

"You're the mother of a young child," she said, "but you're not necessarily young, not in childbearing years."

The trouble is, when you have a child, you're young for each change she goes through, whether or not you're young in child-bearing years. Each new stage is a fresh hell, with too much to learn in too little time, too many mistakes to make that will haunt you in the future—not to mention haunt your child in her future.

————

In the chaos of depression, how does one parent? I collapsed into depression or vibrated with agitation. I might imagine, now, a con-versation with Emma that leads to true communication, but the truth is even without a job I couldn't muster the energy or insight to show up for my daughter back then.

I could not have had a meaningful conversation with Emma because I was sick, and we didn't know it.

What does it mean to be ill and not know it?

When you're physically sick and don't realize it, at some point it shows up. A pain, a rash, a numbness, a malfunction.

It shows up when you're mentally ill, too, but people don't per-ceive it the same way, and you don't experience it the same way.

No one thinks a debilitating migraine is a character flaw. Too many of us believe a depressive's inability to function is exactly that. My family treated my depression as a character flaw because that was how I treated it, and that was because I did not understand the extent to which I was ill. I thought I was flawed, broken, weak, fragile, lazy.

————

I say "my family" and I think I mean my husband and our daughters, but what I really mean, of course, is my parents and my sister.
My sister and I are both neurodivergent. We are not normal. This
is what I want to tell my daughter.

The good news, as I cry with Emma over our noodle bowls, is
that I've learned a great deal about depression over the years, and
I knew I wanted to protect her from ever experiencing it herself.

Of course, I didn't manage that. Not completely. Emma was
depressed during puberty, after a bad breakup with a boyfriend in
college, during an awful entry-level job. But those were situational.
The depression she felt through those experiences was real. But it
didn't last, didn't continue and morph into an impenetrable fog,
didn't require medication or hospitalization. But one thing I am
responsible for was watching Emma closely for signs of depression
like mine.

And that's how I missed other signs of her struggles. I forgot
that, as closely as we are tied, we are not the same person. Which is
ironic, since I was determined not to confuse Emma's individuality
with my own. When she grew to dislike playing the violin, I let
her drop it. When she showed no signs of interest in classic literature, I turned a blind eye to her nightstand filled with mass-market
horror novels. Yet I didn't help her find a substitute for the violin. I
didn't help her find excellent horror reading. I just . . . let her find
her own way.

That approach has a good side and a bad side. I'm proud of
Emma's adult self, of her love for reading, indoor plants, rock
climbing, and vegetarian cooking. I'm not proud that I remained
so often on the sidelines as she developed her interests and made
choices about how to grow up.

I gave both our daughters so much love, but my depression
diminished my ability to provide care for them. I hear this from
Emma as we weep and talk. I did not take care of her then. And

while I can take care of her now, while I can make changes now, that will never undo past neglect. My past neglect. Of her.

This afternoon, this conversation, will forever be burned into my memory because it was the first time I allowed myself to admit my guilt; I had neglected my own child because of my disease— and because of my disease, I didn't realize I was neglecting her. Of course, the actual neglect is worse. However, knowing I didn't even notice it devastates me.

13

THE DIAGNOSIS

After four long months of weekly sessions, my psychopharmacologist says he is ready to speak with me about a diagnosis.

I get behind the wheel. I need to know what is wrong with me.

Houses, schools, subdivisions. Exxon. Package store. Getting closer.

I hate that I need this trip so badly, that I cannot get well, be well, without more intervention. I had hoped, after my latest long stretch of stability, that I was done with adjusting medications. That I was somehow "cured."

I park the battered car. I'm a few minutes early. I flip down the visor, observe the deep circles below my eyes and the rough red patches on my skin, and scrabble through my handbag for cosmetics to disguise them. My hair is lank and greasy, my clothes dark and baggy, but I still want to somehow say, "I care." Do I want to say, "I'm here?" Or am I putting on a mask?

Dr. Rivera is tall, gaunt, and impeccably dressed.

I focus on his Ferragamo loafers.

Today, he is going to tell me something new, something I haven't heard before.

I've put on my mask, at least half of it, so I try to sit up a little, like good girls always do, ready to hear what authority tells us.

Someone else has an answer. Someone else has *the* answer.

I have to believe that. Because, after years and years of treatment for depression, I still don't have an answer. I'm still sick.

MY ILLNESS HAS been misunderstood, carefully tamped down by me, my mother, society's expectations, and the pressures of whatever system/institution I've lived under. As a high school honor student. At a rigorous private women's college. In an overseas military community. As a graduate student, as a new mother, as a middle manager at a large tech company.

People whose lives are undone by fatal illness diagnoses can usually point to an event—a pain, a collapse, an X-ray—when they realized things were never going to be the same. When they knew they weren't going to be all right.

It's not as if I didn't know something was wrong. I had known for very long but couldn't identify it.

I felt like crying all the time at some point every day, and I didn't know why. My mother told my teachers that I was sensitive. My friends called me a crybaby. My sister teased me when I cried, then fell into huge sobbing jags herself. Why? Why was I made this way? Why did the tiniest things make me weep? In church each Sunday the words of the liturgy could bring tears to my eyes: "God so loved the world that he gave his only begotten son." Could I ever do something like that? And if I couldn't, what did I matter?

See, there's the depression talking. I should capitalize *Depression* the way I capitalize *God* because it was just as powerful.

———

Dr. Rivera swivels in his chair, long limbs angled, and picks up my patient file.

"Mrs. Patrick, let's review a few things." He always refers to me as Mrs. Patrick, which I find both respectful and strange—respectful because he is trying to maintain dignity for me as a patient by using my title and surname, strange because even a quarter century after I began using my married name, I'm not accustomed to it.

The doctor reminds me of my initial complaints and symptoms, gives a brief overview of the family history I've provided, and reviews my treatment. "Based on all these, I am diagnosing you with double depression—that is, cycling depression that is a combination of chronic and major episodes."

I must look confused, and I am. What the hell is double depression? I've never heard of it, and I thought I knew more than most people about mental illness and its varieties.

Dr. Rivera goes on to explain that double depression is a form of bipolar syndrome, but instead of bouncing between depression and mania, the person starts out depressed and gets . . . more depressed. If double depression were a story, I think, it would be the most boring one ever written.

But the doctor is still talking, telling me that one of the ways he and his colleagues identify double depression is by looking for severely depressed patients with close family members who have bipolar syndrome. "In some families," he says, "it seems the gene for bipolar affects one child but changes for another child into this kind of depression."

———

In the moment Dr. Rivera offers me this diagnosis, I am fifty-two years old. My sister has just turned fifty. For five decades, I have believed and wished and hoped we were nothing alike. I have been afraid of my sister, enraged by my sister; I've disliked her intensely and yet never been able to disentangle myself from her life and make peace with her until the recent past.

Now I hear information that reminds me we can never be completely disentangled. The two of us are tied together not just by upbringing but by heredity. My diagnosis may be different from hers and my illness's manifestation different, but we both have damaged genes, coded information that makes our brains different. I recall the two of us in our adolescent bedrooms, me weeping while writing journal entries, her dancing while listening to loud music.

Without even considering my sister's other modalities, like borderline personality disorder and schizoaffective disorder, I understand that I cannot view myself as a person affected by mental illness who deserves good treatment, support, and dignity unless I also understand my sister's mental illness that springs from the same sources. If I can be helped, she can too. That doesn't mean the help will be the same or that the outcome will be the same. It just means she also deserves support.

This matters urgently. Not so much that I rush from the appointment to bring my sister tea and sympathy—I don't—but because it snaps me out of the lifelong narcissism of depression. Depressives become narcissists because every minute of every depressed day is spent in contemplation of the self's survival.

For me to think "Ellen and I both need help" was a gigantic step in my recovery, one that receiving a rational, fully considered diagnosis made possible. I was still in the same office, staring at the same doctor's loafers, and yet I was in a new realm. If I could think about what someone else needed, I was definitely ready for a new course of treatment and a new level of health and stability.

———

But receiving a diagnosis also meant that I had been correct. There was a genuine medical issue behind my emotional ups and downs, which were actually downs and downs, low and then lower and even lower. I wasn't weak in character. I didn't have personality issues. It mattered almost less to me that my downs and downs could be changed through medication than it did to learn they existed. It wasn't all in my head. I hadn't been making things up or exaggerating my dark moods for attention.

———

When Adam and I were in our twenties, living in West Berlin, we knew a French couple with whom we became good friends. They invited us to visit their family summer home in Brittany. They'd just had their first baby and were quite busy; the rest of the family had many activities, from sailing to swimming to shopping, to keep them occupied. While we were happy to be left on our own to explore the little beachside town, one day the husband was delegated to send us out on an expedition by boat to Belle-Île-en-Mer, a popular tourist spot.

Our trip was miserable, start to finish. Adam experiences horrible seasickness on the calmest days, and this August morning the Atlantic waters were in turmoil. He spent most of the hour-long ride hanging over the gunwales. Belle-Île appeared anything but belle; it was gray and rainy and rocky and held no charms for the two of us, one queasy and one cranky. Why had we been forced to come here when I could have been happily tucked up in our hotel, reading?

When our friend M. picked us up at the pier in Quiberon, I was more than cranky. I was tired, I was sad, I felt neglected. It would be several years before we had our own first child and understood how desperately new parents can need a day completely free of houseguests. All I understood, as a depressive vulnerable narcissist, is that I was not having a good time, not even an okay time. I've never had much of a poker face. M. took one look at my pouting face and laughed. Before our plane departed a few days later, he presented me with a drawing: Bethanne on the boat to Belle-Île, holding a string that trailed a black storm cloud.

I got the message. I wasn't coming off very well. I'd been seen, and I was ashamed.

———

Receiving a diagnosis that confirmed there might be a reason that I'd come off badly in so many situations for so many years meant I could try to get better, feel some compassion for my sister—and even more important: forgive myself.

As I dragged Storm Cloud Bethanne through La Baule, Brittany's premier resort town, I wasn't trying to impose my tempestuous feelings on anyone else. I know they affected others (especially Adam, at the time). But I wasn't in any control of my feelings in 1988. Things improved when I began taking antidepressants in 1990, but it would take twenty-six years for further improvement.

Twenty-six years is a long time. A long time to feel depressed every day. A long time to wonder why you feel depressed every day. A long time to try and make it through each day doing anything at all, let alone getting clean and dressed and ready and getting two children clean and dressed and ready and then working for eight hours or more and then thinking about meal preparation and homework and activities and then getting clean and into pajamas and ready for bed.

My diagnosis promised improvement. I am all for the idea that we don't need to constantly chase achievement or success, especially as defined by the very late stage of capitalism we're all living through, but I don't think improvement has to mean productivity. We can improve how we communicate. We can improve our spiritual practice. We can improve our macaroni-and-cheese recipe.

Or perhaps what I really mean is this: things can be different.

When Dr. Rivera told me that I have an illness called double depression, when he told me that it could be treated with medication, that there was something to try, I got the message. Things could be different.

———

How could things be different? What would my life look like if things were different?

I'd never wondered. I had no idea. The thing that pushed me to the brink was descending into depression for no reason, meaning there were no external stressors attached to my January 2016 episode, the one that convinced me to ask my physician for a recommendation to a new psychiatrist. I didn't start on my journey to a new diagnosis in the midst of joy, rather in the midst of fear.

Which meant I had a long way to go once I did receive that new diagnosis, and I had no idea how far that way would take me. Just because there's a light at the end of the tunnel doesn't mean the tunnel isn't long; your ability to see that light depends on many factors, including your own eyesight. When I started to feel better in my twenties after taking Prozac, I had no idea that a couple of dozen years into the future I'd be able to feel so much better. I saw a light that was actually a blaze, or at least a good steady bonfire.

———

I was a Girl Scout for years, so I know that the trouble with fires is that they don't always burn steadily. Depending on how you build your initial structure, the wind, the fuel you use . . . so many factors go into a fire's success.

So many factors also go into a person's success, and by success I mean health. Receiving a diagnosis for my illness meant I could take more steps toward being healthy, not merely high functioning.

The term *high functioning* in the realm of mental health means that a person has managed to find strategies that allow her to conduct a life that works—even if it doesn't work particularly well. I'd been a high-functioning depressive for a long time, and it was exhausting. And, unlike many depressed people I know, I wasn't even trying to hide my illness. I didn't talk about it very much, but I did share my struggles with my spouse, my close friends, and my caregivers.

That didn't work very well for me. However, I didn't feel I had a choice (you always have a choice) because I could not explain why I shrugged off so many activities and invitations and responsibilities.

Dr. Rivera and I began meeting on a weekly basis to help me arrive on the path toward genuine health. My new diagnosis was a huge relief, but it also presaged months and years of new, hard work. The work has been as tough and continuous as it might be for a Pilates instructor to maintain their fitness or for a member of the clergy to grow in faith. It's not easy and it's not always pretty. I did not start taking a new medication and immediately turn into my best self.

In the years since learning I have double depression, I've lost a longtime friend, grown closer to our daughters, been rejected by different kinds of editors, been taken on by other editors; I've strengthened my relationship with my husband. Among many other things. The point is that becoming healthy is holistic, and hard, and worth every difficult second.

Once I'd taken antidepressants for the first time, I could see much more clearly. I could experience life without the fog I'd been in for years. After I'd taken an anticonvulsant in tandem with my regular antidepressant medication for the first time, I could feel much more acutely. Not emotions: energy. I wanted to get up off the couch, I wanted to take walks, I wanted to finish tasks.

Depression consumes so much energy. It's a time suck and a self-fulfilling prophecy. With my lowered moods elevated to more

normal (whatever *normal* means) levels, I could understand characteristics I'd observed in other people. Focus. Intention. Joy. I could
feel my desire for those things pulsing from my fingertips, almost as
if tiny roots were shooting out from them. Let's go out for dinner!
Also, let's cook dinner, it will be fun. Yes, I can make it. Also, no,
I'm sorry, that doesn't work for me. Again and again I was making
choices that were new to me. Call it rehab of the psyche. A vic-
tim of stroke or accident spends time and effort on tiny successes
in order to recover. During our sessions, Dr. Rivera would have
me relate current stressors and talk through them with me, not in
a simulacrum of talk therapy (which I was also engaged in on a
weekly basis) but to gently explain how my illness was affecting my
actions and to remind me that I no longer had to use the primitive
tools I'd relied on for so long.

———

Receiving a diagnosis that took into account my genetics, my upbringing, my life choices, and my overall health meant that for the
first time, only my own expectations mattered. What was I going
to do with this new information? How would I handle myself?

For the first time, I decided to trust myself. Not to process the
new information endlessly via phone calls and long conversations
and deep internet dives. To trust myself.

———

No one could present me with self-confidence, that privilege of
privileges, except myself. Some people develop it earlier in life,
and that's wonderful. I didn't have it yet, not enough of it. In order
to have this diagnosis of double depression mean something more
than a new page in my medical history, I was going to have to do
more work.

I've often said to friends who ask me about whether or not to take medications for mental challenges that the chemicals themselves don't make you better. What makes you better is the further growth you're able to pursue once your depression, mania, anxiety, what have you, has been eased. Having fewer low-mood swings once I began taking Trileptal was a second Life B moment, yes; I finally had a day-to-day existence in which I wasn't always depressed.

Having fewer low-mood swings also meant, just as having less depression in 1990 had meant, that I could see more clearly, and seeing more clearly means that you don't just see rainbows and unicorns. You also see flaws in your own behavior. You see relationships that verge on toxic. You see situations that no longer serve your interests. A friend who does the Twelve Steps tells me that facing these challenges is often referred to as an AFGO, or Another Fucking Growth Opportunity.

———

Time for an AFGO. Time for me to use my newly clear perception to change and not just to feel better but to act differently. If I had the chance to live outside of the expectations of others, what would my own expectations be?

I soon realized that feeling better meant nothing if I wasn't learning to treat myself better. Like the proverbial dry drunk, for a period of time after Dr. Rivera's diagnosis, I was completely self-centered, so busy enjoying the relief of stable moods that I didn't bother to change the kind of behavior I'd used for decades while depressed as a crutch.

14

LEARNING TO BEND

EVEN IF YOU'VE NEVER DONE A MOMENT OF YOGA, you're probably familiar with the phrase *downward-facing dog*, which refers to an asana, or posture, performed in nearly every yoga class.

In down dog, a person roots their hands and knees on the mat and then pops their hips in the air while keeping feet on the floor. It's known as a standing rest pose, or an active rest pose, because although it requires limb strength, most of the body can relax through it. Down dog mimics a canine stretch, of course, and at the best of times that's how it should look—like a dog naturally stretching out his front legs.

However, when I began taking yoga in the spring of 2017, I was not even two years out from a total shoulder replacement (TSR). I'd shattered my humerus so badly in a fall up our front step that the orthopedic surgeon, who'd believed he'd be putting in a pin, told me I made him sweat in the operating room like he hadn't done since medical school.

Now that I've broken each limb once, and differently, I can tell you with some authority that it takes several years to fully recuperate from fractures. Exercise a lot, don't exercise at all, the body takes time to adjust, first to the necessary accommodations, then to bones healed to a greater or lesser extent. Eight years after a triple ankle fracture, I'm surefooted again, but as recently as twelve months ago I was still taking extra precautions when going up and down the five stairs between our living room and family room.

When my yoga instructor called out "Down dog" in the second class I attended, I knew what she was talking about. When I tried, I was shocked that I could not do it. I guess I thought my legs would be holding me up, but of course anyone who has performed downward-facing dog understands it requires a lot of shoulder strength.

A lot of shoulder strength.

The next week, and the next, and the next, I tried. My instructor helped me learn an alternate down-dog posture using the wall, which was much easier and helped build up my biceps. I still had a lot of rotator cuff pain, and the problem was that if they corrected it surgically, I'd lose the pain as well as most of the joint mobility.

I continued to push off the wall while my yoga classmates popped effortlessly into alignment. I'm not sure, even three years later, how my twice-a-week instructor managed to look at me, huffing and puffing with effort, my left arm often dangling uselessly as her ballet-toned arms raised and lowered during twists.

Finally, in the winter of 2018, one evening when I was getting ready to stand up and head to the wall, I decided to try popping up, just once more. To my amazement, back went my hips and there I was, supported.

Seconds later I dropped to my knees. It would take another year before I could hold down dog and pedal my heels, another six months after that until I could flow *chaturanga dandasana*. It took a long time. Someone younger, someone stronger, someone healthier, almost anyone at all, wouldn't have needed so much time.

But I needed that much time. If there's anything I've learned during these years aware that I have double depression, it's that healing takes time, and healing can't necessarily be planned.

————

In 2016, my doctor put me on a medication called oxcarbazepine (trade name Trileptal) to control my depressive moods, and my life changed. My constant chronic depression eased. I stopped having so many major depressive dives. My energy, no longer sapped by the hopelessness and despair of negative thoughts, returned to levels that approximated those of an average person.

Martha graduated from high school, and I was there with the rest of the family, fully present, not dragging myself from ceremony to lunch, dreading how low I'd feel. One of the traditions for our area's high school commencements is to present graduates with bouquets. I found a florist to make the most stylish, lush presentation possible, one that I knew no one else would have, to show Martha how proud I was of her achievements and college plans.

That summer I swam and swam at our community pool, spending an hour whenever possible racking up slow laps. It didn't matter how slow they were. I felt like I was swimming back to the surface, returning to a life I'd checked out of involuntarily. Was my reentry voluntary? Mostly. But just because an illness is treated or in remission doesn't mean it's cured, and it also doesn't mean all the symptoms are gone. In the years since my diagnosis, I've gotten better and better. That's the good news. The bad news? There are layers of health. Mental, intellectual, physical, spiritual . . . When you become very, very ill with something like depression, lupus, diabetes, or bipolar syndrome, you often neglect some of the layers of health that can make the difference between surviving and thriving.

I wasn't depressed anymore, but I was irritable. At Martha's graduation lunch, I snapped at my mother for mispronouncing a word. When a friend visited that summer and casually took books from my review shelves, I became furious. Adam began to let me know, in firm tones, when I was being unpleasant. I wasn't nasty to everyone all the time, yet I could feel that my personal setting was on simmer.

With the help of my doctor and my therapist, I started to understand what was happening. When you can suddenly see things clearly after years of blur and astigmatism, you may love some details, and other details may set your teeth on edge. You mean all this time I've been lying in bed, no one was folding the sheets out of the wash? I know I wasn't cooking, but how could you have stocked the freezer with twelve pints of ice cream? I wasn't around for your soccer matches, but that doesn't mean you don't have to listen to me!

I had to recalibrate my vision to accommodate reality. Yes, things around the house were imperfect. Yes, I'd had a tough time making progress in my professional life. Yes, I had to have conversations with my daughters, my mother, my friends. Yes, my marriage needed some care.

But for the first time in years, all those things seemed possible to fix and even change. It might take a while. But it could be done. That was the most important lesson during my first year of healing.

MY PSYCHIATRIST AND I talked about that a lot. "When you take away the illness," he told me, "you always find anxiety. Anxiety is at the root of every mental illness." He cautioned me to pay attention to the anxiety so that I could see what made it better and what made it worse. He didn't want to give me antianxiety medication because it might not interact well with my other medications but also so that I would learn about my anxiety instead of having it fester into something deeper.

Most psychiatrists and psychologists, for billing purposes, note "Depression/Anxiety Disorder" on statements. I'd seen that phrase many times, but I thought anxiety was something that applied to people who couldn't stop jiggling their legs, or people who talked about their worries incessantly, or people who startled at the slightest noise, those nervous types we all see portrayed in movies and on television. I wasn't anxious; I was depressed. I often wished I was energetic enough to jiggle my legs or clean the kitchen obsessively. To me, having anxiety meant having enough energy to care about things.

What I didn't understand is that the times when I had thrown myself into high gear—the times when I excavated the girls' bedrooms in time for a grandparent visit or managed to pack the car properly for a long drive or threw myself into the work required for a deadline—were all periods of anxiety. I rarely did anything in a measured, calm, steady way. I thought it was just natural for me to procrastinate in a moody torpor, then face an ultimatum and meet it, using up so much adrenaline and generating so much cortisol that over the years my always-plump body became just plain obese, more and more overweight the more and more I let things slide and then had to make up for the things I'd let slide.

How I wanted to be more like my friends whose well-oiled households ran like machines. I know one woman who maintains a closet just for her running clothes, each pair of nylon shorts on its own hanger, another whose basement has no more than ten boxes, each neatly labeled. Still another keeps scrapbooks—no boxes of jumbled photos in her house. Even the most eccentric housekeeper I know, whose crowded shelves mix kitsch with children's artwork with priceless family heirlooms, maintains spotless shelves of canned and preserved foods, each labeled according to date and type.

Now, our house was no longer a mess. Once I'd begun the new anticonvulsant medication to combat double depression, I had more energy to keep it in order.

But every little thing that didn't go my way irritated me. I was so angry. Why couldn't everyone keep things tidy? Why couldn't the rest of my family engage in the daily maintenance that made a house a home? I was so angry that I nearly slid back into the listlessness that had defined most of the previous decade. I couldn't do it all on my own, and it felt—*felt*—as if no one else cared.

Martha left for her first year of college. Emma was living in Washington, D.C. Our house was technically an empty nest. And I was technically an utter mess, trying to understand why my life hadn't magically changed with the new meds and new therapist. I published an essay about my diagnosis and got a huge response, but it didn't sink in. I was always on the surface, swimming swimming swimming without a goal or a shore in sight.

WHEN MARTHA RETURNED from her first college year, she told me she'd been doing yoga at the university gym and was amazed at how great she felt after each class. "You should try it, Mom," she said. "I'll go with you."

————

Before entering the studio for that first class, I hadn't been doing much of anything in the way of exercise. Our two elderly dogs were failing and needed fewer and fewer loops around the block before they came home and slouched on the furniture. I was less than a year past my shoulder fracture, my body still in a post-surgical shock, and I had convinced myself the sedentary life was just fine. (Depression lies, and so does anxiety.)

That first yoga class was both more terrible and more awesome than I could have imagined. It was terrible because every muscle on my body shook with effort, while my lungs heaved to maintain the breath necessary for the practice. It was awesome because even while

I was working so hard, my mind felt free for the first time in decades, for the first time since my twenties when I'd gone running every morning. I had to focus on something so effortful that I couldn't grab on to any anxious thought while I moved from asana to asana.

Not to mention the stretched, soothed muscles. But at first those were secondary.

Each time in the three years since that I have taken an easy seat on a mat, whether I am in class or practicing on my own, I take time to center. I'm surprised that yoga isn't required for psychiatric patients, to be honest—the time and effort required to put thoughts aside and focus on breathing isn't just peaceful. It's not just about leaving anxiety behind. It's also about leaving the self behind, and that's revelatory when you've experienced mental illness.

In our culture, mental illness means something is wrong with your mind, and for us, the mind is the center of the self. If the mind is sick, so is the self—or so they tell us. Maybe. Maybe. But what if you can put it all to the side for an hour or more and simply move with your breath? Where is your mind/self then? I don't have big answers. But I did experience big change. My family was at first delighted, then a bit mystified, as I kept going back, twice a week every week, to my local studio—me, who hadn't kept a regular exercise schedule in over fifteen years.

So many people have written about the power of yoga that for me to dwell on it, with my relatively short experience, would be disingenuous. But perhaps I can describe how powerful it was in helping me break through the wall of anxiety that surrounded me. I wasn't just making an effort; I was learning. I could not and still cannot get over the fact that you can practice the same pose for years and it can keep changing your body and your mind and your spirit. As Martha shared, you feel great after a yoga class. But you also feel great the next day, and the next, and you go back to another class and feel great the next day, and the next.

Each time something changes. You make an adjustment. You discover you can take another breath. A muscle builds, and sometimes it's mental muscle. For the first two years of yoga practice, I needed to take huge gulps of water after every sequence. Now, after three years, I might take a drink after a long set of warrior poses, but often I wait until after class to drain my water bottle, because I'm stronger.

You change. Some people like it, even love it. Adam and our daughters saw me interested in something, even passionate about something that wasn't a book. They loved my increased energy and laughter, my improved posture and engagement. My mother applauded my participation in something fitness oriented. Aside from dragging Martha and Emma with me a few times to classes, I didn't proselytize too much; yoga was my thing.

I kept popping into down dog. Sometimes I had to pop right back out. Sometimes I managed to stay in it for a breath or two. Every once in a while I'd return to doing down dog on the wall, on an evening when I'd used my arm and shoulder a lot. I'd done nothing so consistently since practicing the violin through middle school and high school, nothing with so much engagement and joy. Occasionally Adam had to coax me into attending a Wednesday-night class after a long day, but for the most part I looked forward to every class, waking up for Saturday-morning practice at 7:00 a.m. and driving to the studio with an open heart.

Yoga was my choice. Entirely my choice. Not dictated by location or job requirements or parental longing or by a friend's interest. No one made me go to yoga, and no one congratulated me for going either. I could be as lazy or rigid about it as I liked.

When Adam and I were living in Germany in our twenties, I had to make a trip by myself to meet him in France for a military function—he was arriving earlier with his cavalry unit. As a military spouse, I had to travel from Berlin directly to Frankfurt on what we called the duty train, which followed a supervised route through USSR-occupied East Germany. In order to get from Frankfurt to Lyons, our meetup destination, I would have to spend an entire day in Strasbourg.

Those were the days before cell phones or internet. No one knew where I was for an entire day. I got off the train early in the morning and wandered until I found a café open for breakfast: strong coffee and croissants. I walked and walked around Strasbourg, taking in its folksy architecture and verdant landscape, stopping here and there at boutiques selling painted ceramics, lunching on *choucroûte Alsacienne* because I knew that heavy dish would keep me sated until I arrived at Lyons in time for dinner. It was a beautiful day weatherwise and a beautiful day for me personally, eight hours when I wasn't someone's daughter, student, wife.

And later, mother. It would be years before I experienced the freedom of that single day in Strasbourg again, and by then, the world was completely interconnected by digital devices. When I had days (really, evenings) alone in Manhattan while there on business, I could walk along Park Avenue South back to a hotel and say hello to Emma and Martha, asking how their days went. Which was a wonderful thing, a boon for any parent, but so, so different from that single disconnected, anonymous day in Alsace.

Yoga brought me back to that day, because yoga puts you in the present, because yoga connects your body-mind-spirit, because yoga insists that you be you. Stay on your own mat, we are told, and that's not because we disdain connection; it's because we're connecting with ourselves first. Yoga reminds me of how joyful it can be to isolate, especially when you know there's something on either end of that isolation.

I HAVE LIVED a fortunate life in many ways, a privileged life, a life filled with genuine love and affection and connection. Double depression, a mental illness worsened by genetics, upbringing, and stressors, made it difficult, sometimes impossible, to feel that love.

Recently, my sister, who remains very unhealthy but is trying to get better, texted me and said, "I know you're not as manic as I am."

I read that and sighed. No, Ellen. I'm not "as manic" as you are. I don't experience mania at all. She still doesn't understand, or accept, that bipolar syndrome is an illness, like double depression. They're both illnesses, but different illnesses, with different treatment needs. Bipolar mania does not result from stressors, although those stressors can certainly make it worse.

Ellen's new psychiatrist has explained, my mother tells me, that she isn't sure if Ellen has bipolar syndrome or borderline personality disorder. I cannot question the doctor's expertise, but I tell my mother that it is entirely possible for a person to have both a physical illness and a personality disorder at the same time.

I can tell my mother truths like that now because I have become healthy. Not just high functioning anymore, but healthy. I can connect to the love I feel for her, feel her love for me, and also feel her love for my sister. And the love—yes, love—that I feel for my sister.

That love may not look like love to someone who thinks all siblings should be close, or that all siblings should just leave each other alone save for holiday greeting cards. It's love nonetheless. It's a bending, stretching kind of love, a love that adapts to circumstance and needs. It isn't perfect, no more perfect than my Humble Warrior pose (I may never achieve Lord of the Dance pose). But each time I open my heart a little more, answering a text or an email from my sister, it feels different. Not necessarily better or worse. Just different. There's more ease, in both directions. I can bend more forward—or hold back.

And that's okay, both in love and in yoga. No wonder the ancient Greeks (and, probably, other ancient peoples too) had six different words for different kinds of love. Love takes different forms. Loving myself is one of them, and it wasn't until I'd been successfully treated for double depression that I was able to see how sparing I had been with self-care.

When I say self-care, I no longer mean a bubble bath with candles and a glass of wine, although yes, please, whenever. I used to believe that self-care meant indulgence, treats, luxury. I had no one in my life to explain that self-care actually means caring for the self, just as you care for a growing child. To be honest, I wasn't particularly good at caring for growing children, or a husband either. Depression obscured my ability to see the difference between love and care.

When I'm depressed—and yes, I still have depression flares, although they're becoming more rare—my mind tells me that self-care means isolation, stasis, and giving in to the despair that beckons like an enormous soft blanket woven of darkness. If I wrap that blanket around me, depression says I'll be invisible to myself and others.

And depression can come despite medication, treatment, and yoga. Between the fall of 2017 and the spring of 2019, we lost two beloved dogs, plus I lost two of my oldest, closest friends.

———

Grief is a special form of depression, one that almost everyone experiences at some point in their lives. Unfortunately, like all forms of depression, it tricks you into believing that it is the new normal. This is the way things are. My hair, which I was allowing to grow in gray, grew longer and longer and longer. I avoided going to the salon, avoided going anywhere. You'd think, having been there before, that I would recognize what was happening, that someone around me would see what was happening, especially my therapist or my psychiatrist. Right?

Wrong.

Depression's ability to darken life's scrying glass is powerful. So powerful that I didn't realize how low I'd sunk until a friend told me how much she hated my hair. Not that I had any plans to dye it—still haven't, never will—and not that I thought her comments were a kindness, but they did pull me up short with the realization that I hadn't even thought about my hair since my friend's death. I am normally a vain person who worries about things like hair and makeup and clothing on a regular basis. The last time I'd completely forgotten about my hair was after my 1996 miscarriage. Grief. A form of depression. I was grief-stricken.

When you have double depression, you live with the knowledge that you will always have depression. Even when you're well, high functioning and healthy, depression can hit when something unexpected and stressful happens. Grief, for me, can knot things up badly even when I'm medicated and in treatment. Grief, for me, requires careful self-observation and self-care, early disclosure to my support team, and a lot of rest.

As I recovered from those losses, I kept practicing yoga. In the earlier years of our friendship, Frances had been fitness conscious; she hit the gym and the track regularly and didn't understand why I wouldn't, couldn't, join her. I didn't understand then either. I didn't understand that a disease was holding me back, sapping my energy, making it impossible to think about changing into sweats, let alone show up for a workout.

Now here I was, showing up to a studio twice a week for classes that challenged every bone and muscle in my body (even my feet; yoga really changes your feet!). Yoga would never have suited Frances. She was not the contemplative sort. She loved pushing herself in half-marathons and triathlons, not holding a pose for a deeper breath or practicing a heart opener. However, she would have loved seeing me discover a physical activity that suited my temperament, would have loved seeing me stick with it, would have loved seeing me learn to bend.

Bending, I discovered, means much more to me than practicing a stretch until my body lowers another inch. Bending means that I acknowledge that I have a disease that cannot be cured. Bending means that I accommodate my life to that disease. Bending means that I understand that acknowledgment and accommodation are not signs of weakness but signs of strength. One of my favorite phrases yogis use is "If your practice allows," meaning your practice is always evolving. For two years I couldn't wrap one leg over the other to hold a pose. Then, during one class, I tried again and there I was, the sole of my right foot flat on the floor parallel to my left thigh, without effort.

But wait. The important part is that when we switched to the other side? I couldn't do it. My left foot would not stay flat on the floor next to my right thigh that evening. Yet I didn't give up. I picked up my woven strap, wrapped it around my calf, and held myself in the pose. I accommodated instead of giving up.

In the time since Frances died, I have experienced other incidents of depression, thankfully briefer and less intense. "Frequency, intensity, duration," my beloved Father Tim reminds me. "These are the things we try to lessen for a person who experiences mental illness flares." I know I am healthy. I know I am high functioning. I have reduced the frequency, intensity, and duration of my depressive episodes. Yet they still occur. They will continue to occur. I have depression. I have double depression. And I'm okay with that.

15

LITTLE WOMEN

On a balmy January Friday, my younger daughter, Martha, and I decide to go to the movies. We're both anxious to see the new adaptation of *Little Women*, directed by Greta Gerwig. We head to a local cinema, load up on popcorn, Milk Duds, and Diet Cokes, and settle into reclining seats as the screen fills with scenes of nineteenth-century Concord, Massachusetts, and the March family. Each of us cries several times as the familiar story moves forward and backward, sometimes at scenes we expect (when Mr. Laurence delivers Beth's piano, when Colonel March returns home), sometimes at scenes charged with more personal meaning (when Amy steels herself to marry her rich fiancé, when Jo burns her manuscripts).

As we leave the theater, we both sigh contentedly. "That was so good," says Martha.

"So good," I agree. "Although I'll never know why my mother named me after the dead one." I laugh and shake my head.

"Grandma Collier named you after *Little Women*?" says Martha. "I never knew that!"

I nod. "She did, and I always hated that 'my' character dies."

Martha looks at me with one eye cocked. "Mom, you do realize

that Beth is the sister who is the best of them. The character everyone loves the most?"

I slow down. I've never thought of it that way.

IF POSSESSION IS nine-tenths of the law, perspective is nine-
tenths of experience. Like Jo March, I'm a writer, accustomed to
playing with perspective in the pages I create; like Jo March, I often
forget that all the perspectives I create come from my own, and
they're not reliable.

I misunderstood my mother's meaning in naming me Beth.
What else might I have misunderstood over time?

We exited the cinema and walked past coffee shops and boutiques on our way to a new restaurant we'd decided to try. Once we
were seated and had been served delightfully cold cocktails, I took
a good look at my twenty-two-year-old "baby."

First: Thank God she's here. In November 1997 I was nine
months pregnant and lying in bed, working on an article, when
my water broke. It was just like all the books said it would be, a
pop followed by a gush, and just like all the books said, I knew
we needed to get me to the hospital because once the amniotic sac
breaks, you are supposed to deliver within twenty-four hours.

My husband Adam rushed Emma, then only five, to neighbors
alerted for this situation, then bundled my not-inconsiderable bulk
into our station wagon for the drive from our home in Arlington, Virginia, to the National Naval Medical Center in Bethesda,
Maryland. An OB/GYN intern performed a cursory examination
and said we should go home. "You urinated a little," he told me.
"It's not uncommon."

I was furious. I tried to argue with him, but Adam soothed me
and said we should just listen to the doctor and see how I felt the
next day.

I managed to sleep a little, given that we arrived back in the wee hours of the morning to a frightened Emma in the midst of an asthma attack—but by midday Thursday I was having deep contractions. I wandered the house in a bathrobe, trying not to frighten Emma further with moans. By the evening, when my mother arrived so that she'd be available when it really was time to go to the hospital, I was practicing Lamaze breathing and could hardly stand, even though I couldn't bear to sit. The contractions started coming faster and faster.

At 6:00 a.m., I woke Adam from sound slumber. "We need to go to the hospital," I sobbed. "I am in a lot of pain."

This time, the nurses took one look at me and found a wheelchair. The chief of OB/GYN arrived.

"Mrs. Patrick, I'm sorry," he said. "It seems you've been in hard labor since your water broke on Wednesday night. We need to be prepared for an emergency Cesarean in this case, because your water broke over twenty-four hours ago."

I explained that I was told my water hadn't broken.

"Ah, yes, I see that here. But your amniotic fluid doesn't fern in the same direction as most women's does, and our intern didn't understand that."

If I hadn't already been lying on a gurney with a fetal monitor strapped across my abdomen, I might have decked him. But all that mattered from that moment on was making sure my baby lived.

And she did, despite medical negligence. A matter of perspective, the "rational" men around me might've said. She's here, and she is stunningly beautiful. Long, thick, straight blond hair, peachy skin, clear brown eyes, a lovely smile, perfect body, wonderful style and fashion sense.

She looks so little like me, her short, plump, dark-haired mother, that she's been asked if she's adopted. When we remember that, we both laugh, because we are bonded tightly and don't really care what other people think.

But there is something darker and deeper that bonds us too. That something is my history of severe depression.

————

During the week between Christmas Eve and New Year's Eve 2019, we spent a lot of time together as a family, sometimes with both our daughters, sometimes with both of them plus their boyfriends, sometimes just the two of us with Martha. In one of those latter moments, I teased her about a demerit she'd received at an all-girls' summer camp she'd attended. "Leave me alone!" she laughed. "I was just fourteen! My home life was terrible!" More laughter.

Two weeks later, as we dine post-*Little Women*, I need to ask Martha about that sentence: "My home life was terrible!" I'm sure I know part of the answer, but I'm not sure if I should ask. I'm not sure I want the entire answer. I'm not sure that I'm brave enough.

However, I've spent nearly four years on an intense journey out of the depression that began plaguing me in childhood. I'm fifty-six years old and healthy, and if I'm not ready now to understand how my illness affected my closest loved ones, I may never be. I can't force the issue. If Martha doesn't want to discuss the toughest years with me, she doesn't have to.

I TAKE A breath, look into my daughter's lovely eyes, and say, "There's something I want to ask you about, something you may not want to deal with right now." I remind her of what she'd said and explain that, if she's willing, I'd like to hear her perspective on what it was like to grow up with a depressed mother.

She takes her time buttering a piece of bread. She turns her head to the side.

"You don't have to talk about it if you don't want to," I say. I will myself to stop talking, to give her space. It's not a technique I've learned as a journalist. It's a technique I've learned through hard-won experience and more than a little talk therapy.

She blinks rapidly. "I might cry," she says. She knows I don't mind if she cries. She doesn't want to cry in public, doesn't want to cry so hard that she can't talk.

I wait. Then I realize there's something I do need to say.

"I want you to know I'm asking so that I can learn more about you and learn how to be a good mother to you now." I busy myself with my own baguette slice. If you'd seen me, you'd wonder how a piece of crust could be so fascinating.

———

Early in 2016, before I made the decision to talk with the new psychiatrist who would eventually provide my proper diagnosis, Martha came home from her best friend's house and exclaimed, "Quinn's mom helped me write my admissions essay!"

I was—where else?—lying on our living room sofa. After the holidays were over, I'd fallen into a deep depression and couldn't figure out why. I was taking my antidepressant medication, exercising every day, getting work done. But I was badly depressed, thinking about suicide many times each day. I hadn't been able to do much about taking Martha on college visits or helping her with her applications because I'd broken my shoulder in September, although I had managed to go on a trip with her and one of her friends to tour the Five Colleges in Massachusetts; they divided the driving between them.

Now here she was, an essay completed, and here I was, slumped in a disheveled heap. I burned with shame over not being asked by my own daughter to edit her essay—me, the professional writer and book critic. I burned with jealousy that my own daughter asked someone else's mother to help her with college-application material. I summoned a wan smile and said, "That's great. I'm so glad you've got it done!"

Weeks later, after I'd gathered enough courage to ask my doctor for a referral to a psychiatrist specializing in neuropharmacology, I came home and found a stack of pages on the kitchen counter, marked in red pencil. Martha's essay—with her friend's mother's edits.

———

After reading Martha's essay, I felt a combination of shock, cold sweat, and adrenaline. All this time, I'd thought I was maintaining some small pretense of being a real mother, the kind who wasn't ill, wasn't affected by her illness, that maybe Martha thought all mothers were a little distant and fatigued.

But of course she didn't. Why would such a bright teen not notice that other moms didn't spend most of their time holed up in the bedroom? Why wouldn't she see that other moms didn't have to be coaxed to the dinner table by their partners, that other moms talked and asked questions instead of staring at their plates and eating fast so they could return to their beds?

What Martha didn't know, couldn't know, was that I was a member of what is now sometimes known as spoonies: people with chronic, debilitating diseases like Epstein-Barr syndrome, lupus, and, yes, depression, who know they can only do a limited number of things in each day, those things represented, say, by spoons. If you know you have to go to work, that might use up three of your five spoons; the remaining two are allotted to buying groceries and putting the kids to bed. Those of us who identify with this description know from the start that we can't do it all. We can't even do most of it.

However, when you have lupus, you can tell people, and they make accommodations for you. You have a Real Sickness, one that limits you—but family and friends and colleagues understand it. They can wrap their minds around physical ailments. They can't wrap their minds around mental ailments.

Until the moment I picked up Martha's essay, I'd been so busy making sure most people didn't have to wrap their minds around my mental illness that I hadn't noticed my family had been dealing with it all along. I could go to an office and sometimes keep my depression at bay. I could attend a meeting with a teacher or a doctor and appear "normal." But at home, where the laundry piled up so high we called it the laundry mountain, where I rarely answered the door let alone picked up the phone, there was no appearance of normalcy. My husband picked up the pieces as best he could, but my daughters had a very sick mother, a mother who could not function in a healthy way as a parent.

———

Here's how a mother who could not function in a healthy way looked, at least to Martha: "You never did anything for me," she said as we waited for our meal to arrive. "You didn't cook. You never did the laundry. You didn't come to any of my soccer games. When my friends came over you were always in bed. I thought you hated children because you never talked to any of them."

I want to reach across the table and hold her, this child of my heart whose fetal distress once made me say firmly, "I'll have the Cesarean now; there's no need to wait another twenty minutes." I want to tell her about the years before she can remember, when I did cook, every single night; when I not only did the laundry but ironed the dishcloths too; when I organized complicated birthday parties for her older sister, like the Harry Potter–themed one where we made chocolate-dipped pretzel wands and had a Quidditch match in the backyard; when I tried so hard to make other mom friends I would lose when we moved. Again.

———

But since my diagnosis of double depression, I've learned a great deal. I've learned that I am not one and the same with depression, that I am a whole person without that illness. I've learned that the anxiety underlying all forms of mental illness must and can be dealt with. I've learned that without depression and anxiety, a person can gain psychic and physical strength that leads to being healthy, not just high functioning.

Most important, I've learned that the depression that felt, to me, like isolation affected the people I love the most—and that their experience is just as, if not more, important than mine in my new life, a life in which I am able to connect with those loved ones in meaningful ways.

As Martha speaks, I listen. I don't try to make excuses or apologies. I don't try to tell my side of the story. I listen, and it is tough to hear, but things were much tougher for Martha as she grew up.

"I think I'm a feminist because Dad did everything," she says. "Everything. He was the only parent I could rely on. He checked my homework. He made my lunch every day. He watched television with me after you went to lie down. He drove me and my friends to the movies."

Finally, I do interject. "I think it's hard for you to understand some aspects of my life with your father, some of the decisions he made for his career that affected me, affected my chances of a career, and those decisions contributed to my depression."

Wrong answer. She gives me a steely look and says, "You knew what you were getting into when you married someone in the military."

Now that I've become healthy, I know when it's time to stop, or at least pivot. Our daughter isn't ready, or willing, to understand that the currently strong marriage her father and I share isn't the same marriage we always shared, or that it might have affected me mentally. I remind myself that this conversation is about her and her experience of my parenting when I was unhealthy.

But I have so many things I want to tell her, things I don't think I could describe properly to therapists, things that would be unintelligible to those who didn't live under that same roof. I want her to know what it was like to grow up in a house where my maternal grandmother lived upstairs and was never spoken to or spoken about, to grow up with parents whose psyches were twisted by the mental illnesses of their elders, to know that my only sibling, my sister, was off, to get through several levels of schooling despite suicidal depression, to be a wife and mother with the same, to know that more than anything, more than anything, once I had my children to hope more than anything that they would escape my disease, the disease I tried so hard to hide—and failed so miserably at hiding—from the rest of the world.

————

During both my full-term pregnancies, I was happier and calmer and less moody than at any other time in my life before my 2016 diagnosis. During both pregnancies I took Prozac, though I took the same dose before and after each pregnancy. While I was pregnant, my brain felt better. Those months of pregnancy convinced me that it was possible to feel healthy and contented and not think constantly of self-erasure and/or self-harm.

Emma had five years as an only child, five years when I was still deeply depressed but had only one little soul in my care. I tried so hard in those five years to become the perfect mother I thought I was supposed to be, a woman who raised her child without resorting to day care, a woman who provided meals for her little family, a woman who kept her child dressed in bandbox-perfect clothing and hosted playdates and made low-sugar birthday cakes from scratch.

Emma, there are so many things I want to tell you, so many things you'll never ask, so many ways I've hurt you, so many painful episodes between us.

If I could write this story as a novel, if I could take you, my own little woman, into a fictional realm, I would write a story about a mommy who cares less about the rest of the world than about her own family, a mom who may be ill but has people who support her in finding the right kind of treatment for her illness earlier, a mother who perpetrates so much less damage in her wake.

16

CAREFUL PRUNING

I HAVE A FRIEND WHO LIVES ON GRAND ARMY PLAZA in Brooklyn in a wonderful old building with a doorman, a hand-operated elevator, and a view over treetops toward the phenomenal Brooklyn Public Library.

Occasionally when my friend is away on business I move in, and among the pleasures on offer (Four and Twenty Blackbirds pie slices at the library coffee shop, half a block's walk to the F train, Prospect Park across the street), the greatest is the very short walk to the Brooklyn Botanic Garden. Past the modest gates lies a carefully planned and tended nirvana of florabundance, including a northeast woodlands section, roses of every imaginable kind, a Japanese contemplation garden, and even a space for teaching children about sustainable agriculture.

Tucked away behind two large lily ponds is a glass greenhouse devoted to the Japanese art of bonsai, a word that means "tray planting" but has come to stand for any and all miniature trees and bushes. I always take a long, considering stroll through the greenhouse; I've always loved the twisty asymmetrical bonsai trees in their low ceramic pots.

———

When I was visiting the bonsai last summer, I took the time to read a placard near the entrance: through careful pruning, bonsai cultivators convince the trees that they are up to thirty feet tall—even though their actual heights are only three to five inches.

Remember that little ding of recognition you felt when you met your first best friend? That's the same ding I experienced reading that sign. No, I don't think I'm thirty feet tall. However, I do know that I owe the beautiful and lush foliage of my current life to an extensive root system developed through decades of pruning: sometimes cut back, sometimes allowed to flourish.

———

I am one of those people who has always felt a strong sense of the divine. My earliest memories of churchgoing include the feeling that I was connecting with God—and that connection helped through a childhood when I often felt despair.

One of the reasons, I now understand, that I experienced despair is because I suffer from depression, have suffered from depression since those earliest memories. At the time I had no idea what depression was; all I knew was that I regularly and keenly felt deep, deep sadness, sadness untethered to anything happening in my daily life. Although there were hard things in my family history, my periods of heart-wrenching doldrums as a young child had little to do with them.

Or, perhaps, they had everything to do with them.

———

Where the sadness in my genes, the roots, has been met by trauma, the pruned branches, is where my depression can be most plainly observed. My greatest weakness has, in the course of my life's journey, become my greatest strength.

I believe that everyone's greatest strength is also their greatest weakness. If you're imaginative, you're also prone to losing track. If you're compassionate, you're probably also an easy mark. If you're determined? Stubborn. Detail oriented? A dreadful perfectionist. And so it goes.

It also works vice versa. Always tardy? You're likely incredibly observant. Stingy? Parsimonious. My genetic tendency toward cycling depression, magnified by setbacks I experienced, is also the source of my deep understanding of suffering. Robin Williams said, "I think the saddest people always try their hardest to make people happy. Because they know what it's like to feel worthless and they don't want anybody else to feel like that."

———

When I collapsed into tears as a child, it was often because my parents were fighting—a very common reason for children to cry. My parents fought about money and other resource allocations, from large appliance purchases to car repairs to who would pick whom up from which after-school activity (the answer was usually my mother, in her fairly traditional role as primary parent).

Maybe they fought too often, too much, too hard. They didn't have much room in which to conduct their battles; there were just a few feet between our living room and kitchen and their bedroom. Some Manhattan tenements are larger than our living quarters were. What were the married parents of two small children who had a mother-in-law living upstairs supposed to do?

———

Many stories about illness follow a familiar trajectory. A happy, fulfilled person received a wonderful education, found a partner, began a career, started a family—and then discovered a lump/ limp/bruise/stutter that presaged a terrible, often terminal, illness or disease. I am not making light of those stories; they are important and necessary.

But my story has a different trajectory: the author was a miserable, terribly ill person who got a wonderful education, found a partner, began a career, started a family—and finally, finally got better.

Getting better is a wonderful thing, but it doesn't make my trajectory better or worse. What my trajectory does mean is that my illness affected my education, my partner, my family, my friends, my career. So my story has to be told differently. My story can't focus closely on weeks, months, or years of illness; it has to be told through a wider lens. But it still needs to stay focused on me, because I'm the one who's been ill; I'm the one whose illness has touched all these other people.

In my bonsai life I have often been the pruner as well as the pruned, choosing to cut myself off from new growth. Good pruning can help a bonsai plant deepen its root system and develop an aesthetically pleasing growth pattern. Bad pruning can have the opposite effects.

I don't always prune particularly well. I spent weeks and months of my college years shut away in my room, skipping classes because I was tired (read: depressed) and unprepared (read: depressed). The one time I went to the clinic and asked for mental health care because my stomach hurt constantly (a GP screened me for internal issues), I was given a prescription for phenobarbital and told to consider a long vacation somewhere warm. I continued skipping class, curling up with copies of *Vogue* and bags of Hershey's Kisses on my hard single bed.

Another bad pruning incident: I decided, against my then psychiatrist's advice, to pursue pregnancy. I wasn't well. I wasn't ready to be a mother. I was at my wit's end at failing (or so I saw it, since I never actually applied) to be granted entry to my university's doctoral program; I was determined to progress in some area of my life. The good girl's default: when in doubt, show your progress. I was following life's instructions for overachievers, attempting to gain a gold star in parenthood even though what I really wanted was the floppy cap of a newly minted PhD.

However, I've made some good pruning decisions too. I may have rushed into marriage for the wrong reasons, but I married the right man—which I can prove by showing you pictures of a recent vacation, thirty-two years in, the huge grins on our faces, completely at ease with each other. The three-plus decades we've been together have not been perfect, but they've been meaningful. There is no one else I'd rather be with. We might be a little too hermetically bonded; we could use more of a social life. But the roots and branches on my psychic bonsai representing our marriage are strong and healthy.

More good pruning: Once I realized I needed to be medicated for depression, I made sure I continued to be medicated for depression. Wherever the army moved us, I found a psychiatrist and/or a physician who would prescribe psychiatric meds. I intuitively realized, long before I rationally understood, that I could not cope without chemical support.

———

I am not thirty feet tall. I barely clear five foot two. But because I have not stopped seeking treatment, because I have not accepted one reality to mean all realities, my gaze can clear the tops of redwoods.

My story is my struggle to overcome double depression. No, back up. My story is how I learned to overcome double depression, because I had to teach myself, again and again, not to settle. That isn't easy. Bonsai plants can live from one hundred to five thousand years. Five. Thousand. Years. That makes my five decades or so of life look like a tiny inkblot.

When I was depressed, a thought like that would have cut me off at the knees. My life, a tiny inkblot, meant that I was insignificant. That feeling of insignificance is one of my earliest wounds, and try as I might with therapists and spiritual directors and psychiatrists and close friends, I do not precisely know why. I may never know why. In dark moments—which I still have, but far less frequently than I once did—I believe that I am not just insignificant but inconsequential. Oh, why stop there, says my depression? You're not just inconsequential—you're actually a blot on the sun. The world would be better off without you. Your family would be better off without you.

And then I think, snarkily, Depression's a pretty poor substitute for a killer disease. If depression was as dangerous as they tell us, why am I still alive? And then, It's not depression that's weak. It's you. You're so useless, so worthless, that you can't even manage to kill yourself. You have everything you need: A shelf of dangerous medications. A drawer full of well-sharpened knives. Razors and a deep tub. Rope and a high attic ceiling with crossbeams. Two cars and a poorly ventilated garage. Just get on with it, can't you?

Inaction becomes its own form of action. You can't swallow or cut or sway, so you breathe and cry and cry and cry and cry and cry and cry. You are a complete and utter failure. You will live to see tomorrow.

———

Not everyone sees tomorrow. As I write this, a friend's husband has died by suicide. A man in his late fifties, he left a grieving spouse and daughter. Well, a separated spouse. My friend left him a few years ago because she could not live with him; he refused treatment.

Many of us with mental illnesses refuse treatment, even if only for short periods here and there. Some of us try everything and nothing works: That was the case for an old friend of my husband's, who hanged himself in his bedroom closet at his parents' house. He'd moved there because, years after first suffering a bout of major depression, he knew he needed their support.

Sadly, the truly hopeless will always find a way to end things. They cut themselves off from relationships and passions and beauty, not pruning with care but hacking away at any roots that keep them tethered to a world they find unbearable.

I know how it feels to find the self and the world unbearable. Yet somehow—and sometimes through the very people and events that wounded me—I found myself, in my darkest hours, firmly rooted in healthy soil. Parts of my psyche might have withered, but I still had rich reserves on which to draw. Overcoming double depression means that I had to use everything at my disposal to gain self-knowledge and self-worth, enough of both so I could become a strong self-advocate. You can be supported by the rich soil of love and pruned by the patient soil of treatment, but only you, the person with mental illness, can do the growing.

So you fail at suicide and succeed at surviving. What next? How do you handle this growing, by which we really mean this living? Some say, "You can bear anything for ten seconds"; others exhort you to live "one day at a time." Maybe those maxims annoy you (they often annoy me), but when it comes to illustrating how slowly growth happens for the mentally ill, they're completely accurate. You can't see the leaves of a bonsai tree unfurling. You can't see a person recover from treatment-resistant depression.

Yet when I return to the Brooklyn Botanic Garden—maybe this year, maybe next—I know that the bonsai house will contain all sorts of new growth. Thankfully, so will I.

17

FAMILY ALBUMS

I SIT ON MY MOTHER'S DAYBED, AWKWARDLY PROPPED up with pillows so that I can cover as much space as possible with piles of photographs, mostly snapshots, family pictures, some of them neatly organized in albums and binders, many more lose in cardboard and plastic boxes. All told there must be a few thousand photos for us to sort through, my mother and me.

Mom lived alone from 2006 when my father died until early 2021. She weathered the global pandemic in 2020, keeping up social ties by having conversations with various neighbors when she went on her daily walks, but in her near-fifteen years of widowhood her world shrank rapidly, and in some ways deliberately. Mom seemed to like fewer and fewer things—people, organizations, sports, community. If this was a form of depression, she didn't want to discuss it. She was fine. Period. She was living as she wanted to, and maybe, just maybe, after a lifetime of caring for people when she was too young for that or not ready, she meant it: she wanted to be alone.

Of course, we saw her several times a year. Summer vacations at the Cape or in New York State. Thanksgiving, then Christmas. Spring breaks/Easter holidays. Memorial Day or July Fourth weekends. But that didn't mean I became more comfortable spending long stints of time with my mother, or she with me. We functioned best when there were other family members around, people to organize things for or pay attention to, and besides, I was busy with work and children and my own depression, too mired in my own muck to encourage Mom to try anything new or talk about her own needs and feelings.

I MANAGED TO find a proper diagnosis and good treatment for my mental illness. I found ways to become physically and emotionally healthier, more stable. I began to grow and develop as a writer. That's a lot of change—good change to be sure, but a lot.

I needed to get through those changes before I could address something just as important: my relationships with family members. In 2020, I urged my mother to stay put and not travel, admitting only to myself that I was getting off easy without her visits. Less time around her anxiety. Less time spent scouring every corner of the house so it would meet her eagle-eyed scrutiny. Fewer conversations about my sister's various dilemmas.

But as the new year rolled in, Mom and I started talking more seriously about the need for her relocation. After a difficult few months selling the house where my sister, her ex-husband, and their son lived and finding a townhouse for them to move into, my mother admitted she was ready to move. She was tired of being isolated, as well as of taking care of the house and garden/yard by herself. But she wanted to take the transition slowly, maybe moving in a year, or two years.

Those careful plans were upended by her long-term-care insurance policy, which dictated a large premium if she didn't begin residency in an assisted-care facility by her eighty-fifth birthday. Money is Mom's great motivator, and before any of us could give her advice, she'd placed the family home on the market and begun the agonizing process of decluttering the house she'd lived in for nearly sixty years.

Several people helped with the local stuff, like furniture, minor repairs for the new owners, and landscaping tasks. My sister and her family took a weekend off and made many trips to the nearest land-fill with once-precious possessions that no one wanted anymore. But when I offered to do the same, Mom asked me to wait. "Find a weekend when you can come and help me with pictures," she said. "That's something I need you for that only you can do."

Adam knew I needed him with me for a long weekend when we'd say goodbye to a house and region so important to us both. Since his parents had moved to Florida in 2018, we weren't sure when, if ever, we might make a trip back to the Hudson Valley. We decided to spend Memorial Day weekend in New Windsor. Adam would pack the entire kitchen while I sorted through the family photographs.

We arrived on Thursday afternoon and decided to start work on Friday, spending the afternoon recovering from the drive and the evening enjoying an outside pizza dinner at a favorite place in the next town over. Before we'd even opened a bottle of wine (Mom doesn't drink much, and rarely, but she and Adam enjoy sharing the red wine I don't tolerate well), I could tell something was different. My mother was relaxed in a way I'd never seen her before, at ease with us, clearly happy to be in our company, relieved that we'd arrived. The three of us ate and drank and laughed in the spring dusk, the way I'd always hoped I would with my family, which never seemed to happen when my father was alive, before my sister and I grew up and moved away.

If you have never participated in winnowing someone else's artifacts, you may not be prepared for the sheer glut of ephemera the average four-person American family can generate. My mother had eight to ten large moving boxes filled with photos, enough piles to make me briefly wish we'd bought Eastman Kodak stock back in the day.

But we had a plan. We decided that first we would choose the photos Mom wanted to have digitized, made shareable; after that, we'd make stacks for individual family members, including her cousin Gwen, the only first cousin with whom she maintained close contact.

As Adam cranked up tunes through his headphones and wrapped dishes and pans, Mom and I started sorting. It was a much slower process for her than it was for me, especially because she has more memories of some of the older relatives I never knew well. I was nervous that this process would cause her to become weepy or overly sentimental about some of those relatives.

The surprise: you never know when someone is ready to let go. Maybe none of us know when we're ready to let go. Mom was ready to let go. She and I worked steadily and with constant conversation, making decisions and remembering events and people. "That was on the patio," and "When did she leave for Australia?" and other questions that wouldn't mean anything to anyone except the two women in that room.

My mother could rely only on me for this task, and she is the only one for whom I'll ever do such a task. The winnowing of a person's possessions follows, unsurprisingly, the winnowing of a person's connections. Many people—although not all—lose friends and family members in increasing proportion to their age. Due to multiple factors, from geographical separation to deliberate estrangement to apathy, my mother at this point had few people with whom to share her life's highlights.

Sifting through the piles of pictures, I was brought up short: Where were all the ones of me and my sister as babies, toddlers, schoolchildren? Our father had been an inveterate photographer, first with a beloved Brownie camera and then on to increasingly complicated models. One of the last places he visited before his illness left him reliant upon a wheelchair was the local camera shop, Monell's, where he loved to stop in, see the latest models and lenses, and chin-wag for a bit before heading to the Greek donut shop for a sandwich.

I have a very good memory. It's even a bit eidetic. I can remember things like the contents of a closet or a drawer, which side of the page a particular paragraph is on, the order of shops on a main street. I remembered, and clearly, several boxes of black-and-white snapshots, the kind with the wavy edges, snapshots of us as children with aunts and uncles and cousins, snapshots of us as beloved babies, snapshots of birthday parties and holidays and orchestra concerts.

Where had all of them gone?

I asked. "Mom, where are all of the old black-and-white photos?" She shrugged. "I'm not sure which ones you're talking about."

It wasn't until a couple of months ago that I sat up straight one day in my office chair and thought: My sister took them. My sister has those photos. For all I know, she might have lost or destroyed them. That was why they no longer existed in Mom's house, why she gave me such a vague answer.

Making progress yourself is just that. You make progress. You can't control anyone else's. Some people make progress, evolve, heal, move on, and others don't, and the reasons they don't are as varied as the reasons you did.

When I realized that the photos had been taken, I was angry. For about two minutes.

Then I remembered how many photos had still been available to send to the digital-archive service. I remembered how much fun Mom and I had choosing them, laughing over the enormous colorized mid-1960s family portrait in which everyone's cheeks were the same dubious pink. I remembered that we'd been able to include pictures of everyone we loved, everyone most important to us.

And I remembered that even if we'd had far fewer images, we still would have enjoyed the task of organizing them. For the first time that I remember, my mother and I were constructing a family narrative together, with our whole hearts. We weren't going at it or giving each other the silent treatment (my mother is better at that than I am, not because I am a better person but because I am too anxious to endure that kind of silence for long).

My sister is, of course, in the digitized photos, all the way through. I saved a couple dozen pictures for her, separate from the others, photos of her ex-husband with some of their friends, for example.

She's also in the much, much larger box that I am now in charge of. Someone, somewhere, might have other files with pictures of my father's family, but since his was also small, I am now the keeper of his baby album. And his grandfather's photographic record of his World War I service, complete with riding jodhpurs and bivouacs but without captions or names. The handful of snaps from my maternal grandmother's premarriage flapper days, the elaborate portraits of my paternal grandmother's cosseted New England childhood. The sepia-toned wedding portrait of my maternal great-grandparents, clearly affluent at the time, somewhere in Krakow, Poland.

It's all bits and pieces. Even if I had the will to comb through genealogical sources, our family trees have lots of broken and missing branches. Just because people lived in times when it was possible to record their existences doesn't mean those records exist. Some people are given to organizing and arranging. My mother had several albums into which she'd painstakingly glued maps, tickets, receipts, postcards, and photos of trips she'd taken—but photos of landscapes don't mean much to anyone besides the travelers. Our daughters, true Gen Z-ers that they are, don't want to keep Grandma's albums. They'd rather have photos of Grandma in their own albums.

Some money may come to us one day from my mother. Not much. Which doesn't matter. By passing along these memories to me, she is deeming me not her one true inheritor but the caretaker of the family story.

Anyone who ever has done this kind of task will recognize how exhausting it is. Mom and I, for three days, fall into a sensible rhythm. We work from eight to twelve, break for lunch, break for naps (which I need as badly as she does), work again from two until five, and then tidy up the room before dinner and whatever relaxation suits us.

Our eyes get tired, but so do our psyches. More than once our eyes fill with tears on seeing a silly photo of my father. Pictures that I sent over the years, before and after my daughters were born, remind me of times when I was well and functioning, times when I was ill and unable to do much beyond the bare minimum.

For the first time, I am not trying to separate myself from the people in this ragtag collection. I am, instead, trying to find what connects me to them, without unhealthy enmeshment. I'll never have fond memories of one aunt the way my mother does, and that's all right. Just because I don't remember her fondly doesn't mean her photo doesn't belong in this collection.

The same goes for both my grandmothers, the women with whom I began my journey toward understanding what it means to be a woman with mental illness. Both of them were loved and reviled by different people, people who didn't understand, and in some cases didn't try to understand, what was happening to them.

I have so few pictures of either one. Neither kept a journal, or a diary, or even, as far as I can tell, saved a wall calendar. I don't know much about their daily lives, and I never will. I don't know anything about their early dreams or early disappointments either. My mother doesn't, and neither did my father. The one person who might have been able to tell me something about Grandmother

Collier would have been Uncle Matthew, who lived with her for her entire life. Now he is gone. Grandmother Wojcik left no possessions behind; I still find it difficult to bring her up with my mother, due to both our sets of complicated feelings around a woman so troubled.

First we find my grandmother Collier, whose face I have only seen in her childhood portrait photographs and in my memories of her as a woman in early old age. Here she is, in glued-down snapshots carefully placed in my father's baby album. "Emily, Lake Zoar, Connecticut." Suddenly she's neither a spoiled dressed-up daughter of a rich man nor a bewildered elderly lady in corduroy bedroom slippers. In these pictures, my paternal grandmother delights in her oldest son's play during a holiday, her head thrown back in genuine laughter, her thick dark hair held back with a clip.

My father was born in 1930, his brother in 1932, so if my father is already a young toddler in these photos, my grandmother must have been pregnant with her second child at that time. It would be just months until she gave birth and suffered the postpartum depression that would send her, along with my infant uncle, into a mental hospital. The great family secret that perhaps should never have been a secret—but it was.

My mother may never understand how important seeing these photos is to me. She believes that I am attached to Grandmother Collier because she was better off and better educated than Grandmother Wojcik. She is wrong. I think I related more to Grandmother Collier because I sensed her malaise as my own. I knew what it was like to feel sad, to have very little energy.

But I didn't want to be just like Grandma Collier any more than I wanted to be like Grandma Wojcik. There are even fewer images of Sofie Wojcik than there are of Emily Collier, only one of my mother and Aunt Ann with both their parents. In that photo

both Grandma and Grandpa Wojcik are seen from the side, walking toward something, their faces hardly visible.

Finally, there's a small black-and-white, actually sepia, snapshot
of Sofie. On the back is written "Sofie and Clara, 1929." Definitely
before she had children, definitely before she married Jan Wojcik
in 1930. My grandmother is standing on a street, no doubt in Newburgh, New York, her hair cut in a distinct 1920s bob, a cloche
over it, her lips set firmly, her legs shapely from the miles of daily
walking she did throughout her life, perhaps in part to calm her
inner demons. Clara also sports a bob and a cloche, but there's one
significant difference: she is Black. The easy way the two women
are standing indicates friendship, and in 1920s Newburgh, friendship between a white person and a Black person would not have
been common, or necessarily easy.

I have so many questions about these photos of my grandmothers. Who else was on the trip to Lake Zoar? Did my father's
father take the photographs, or was my Grandmother Collier taking her son to visit a teaching colleague? When did she find out her
husband was going to move their little family from New Haven
to New Jersey? She was happy on that particular day, but had she
previously experienced depression? Did she have any hint of what
was to come in her life?

What about my grandmother Wojcik, who on that day in 1929
would have been called Sofie Piekarsz, or Newman? What were
her hopes and dreams? She had other sisters who had married, one
to a reliable if stolid man, the other to the kind of violent alcoholic
Sofie herself would later find. Did she consider marriage her only
future, or did she want something else? How and when and where
did she meet Grandfather Jan, and what did they do for fun on
their days off? Was my grandmother already riding a roller coaster
of moods, or was that something that would affect her after she'd
had children?

But no matter how much or how little I learn about either one of my grandmothers, what I'm learning as I sit and sort photographs with my mother is that our feelings may be complicated, our relationships may be complicated, but things have finally changed. I am healthy and stable and can appreciate my mother's love and care for her family, as well as carry on the love and care for my father's family. I can see myself as both part of, and separate from, the family connections that make up our particular story.

The final box of photos for me to take home was so heavy that all three of us had to carry it out to the car, Adam and me holding up opposite sides, my mother guiding us down steps to the car trunk. It still needs to be unpacked and properly shelved. But I am the steward of this fragile little cardboard ship, the person who needs to somehow make sense of its contents. Or give up on it.

I HAVE THAT choice.

I have always had a choice, and it turns out that I made one too. I thought I experienced two versions of how to be a woman with a mental illness, but there were actually more versions than I thought, and anyway, I've made my own. I've inherited a lot of strength from many different people, and in separating from my family's narrative, I've found a way to write myself back into that narrative.

I wish I had more pictures of my grandmothers. I wish I knew more about what they loved and enjoyed, what they dreaded and feared, how they saw themselves. My family's albums are incomplete, for many reasons. When my grandmothers were young, photography was expensive, a luxury. When they grew old, the cameras were focused on the young, the children in the family.

Even if I never get all the photographs in order, I will be able to make connections between them. I will be able to tell our daughters who the subjects are, why they matter, and something about our connections to people nearer or farther in the past.

Most important, I will share more than just the connections, achievements, and milestones. I will share some of the pain too. I will acknowledge the struggles people like my grandparents and my parents and others experienced. And I will tell the story of how I, a woman who has a mental illness, learned to get the support, treatment, and knowledge I needed to accept myself and live in the world.

Acknowledgments

Like my career path—which has not followed any of the traditional publishing arcs—this book's journey has been unusual. Please bear with me as I thank people from all the steps in the process.

Life B began on a dark fall evening in Northampton, Massachusetts, after an event and drinks with novelist Meg Wolitzer, when author Cathi Hanauer said she was having a tough time finding someone to write an essay about taking psychiatric medication for her second anthology, *The Bitch Is Back*. I said I'd love to write one for her, on spec. She agreed, I wrote an essay, and we went through a couple of rounds of edits before mutually deciding my piece didn't fit.

Later that summer, Allison Wright invited me to the *Virginia Quarterly Review* Writers' Conference to present on a panel; for my sins, I was offered the chance to take part in essayist Rachel Kaadzi Ghansah's nonfiction workshop. Not only did that workshop help me reimagine my essay; I met writer Katie Rose Guest Pryal, whose honesty and authenticity about her own mental health struggles gave me strength to keep working on the piece.

I spent months trying to craft a proposal for a book about bookishness, but when my agent Howard Yoon asked me to share with him something I really cared about, I sent him my essay about taking medications and depression. An hour later, he called and said, "This is what you need to be working on," and told me he was going to send it to Chloe Schama, then at Elle.com. Many thanks to Howard and Chloe for seeing what was urgent (and what was not!) in my piece, and to Chloe for publishing it on Elle.com.

"I Will Always Be Depressed, and I'm OK with That" came out in September 2016 and went viral-ish. Howard encouraged me to work on a new book proposal. It took a while, by which time the Ross Yoon Agency had hired the wonderful Katie Zanecchia as an associate agent. Katie held my nervous hand through the submission process, and we sold *Life B* on proposal to Dan Smetanka at Counterpoint Press in August 2017.

Dan is a dream editor, both because of the magnificent list he has built at Counterpoint, and because I knew how loyal his authors are to him. Thank you, Dan, for seeing something in my proposal—and for seeing it through. Your edits are brilliant, thorough, and clear.

Thank you to Counterpoint editor (now editor at large) Jennifer Alton for our two years together, and your listening to my long, complicated-but-not-brilliant thoughts about depression.

Thank you to everyone at Counterpoint, like uber publicist Megan Fishmann and her team, especially Alisha Gorder, who believes in *Life B* and will deserve a huge basket of chocolate when we're done. Thanks to Dana Li for their beautiful, nuanced cover design. Thank you to Rachel Fershleiser at Catapult, the Counterpoint Press mama bear company, and her marketing geniuses. Many thanks to Laura Berry and her production team; every writer needs an editor, but also a copy editor, a proofreader, and maybe several others I don't know about as well.

When I decided that *Life B* would be a memoir that did not include a story about my work in publishing, Howard and I decided I would be best off with a new agent. Switching agents midcontract is not common, but Howard helped me transition to working with Jennie Dunham of Dunham Literary without so much as a blink. Much appreciation to both of them for the great professional acumen.

Jennie Dunham has shepherded me through writing the third and fourth drafts of *Life B* and supported me as I wrote five new chapters during one three-week residency in late 2021 at the Virginia Center for the Creative Arts, or VCCA (fellow artists, you need to apply). Without VCCA, you would not be reading these acknowledgments. Namaste, everyone in Amherst, Virginia. Special shout-outs to Kate Kazin, Mary Bonina, Gregg Wren, Jon Pineda, and Garrard Connelly.

Thanks to literary star Chuck Adams, formerly the editor in chief of Algonquin Books, who helped me get through a tricky stage in revision.

Thanks to my beta readers Sarah Sandman, Susan Coll, and Michael Taeckens.

———

Thank you to Carol Fitzgerald of *Bookreporter* for allowing me to write some of my earliest book reviews.

Thank you to John Hogan of the late, great *PAGES* magazine, for allowing me to become the first and only telecommuting staff member/editor at large, from 2001 to 2005. For *PAGES* I interviewed authors like Sue Grafton, P. D. James, oh, I can't even remember them all. It was a heady introduction to the literary community for an isolated military spouse who lived in the middle of Texas. Here's to more steakhouse hopping, JMMH!

When we returned to the east coast, it was the aforementioned Carol Fitzgerald who helped me jump into a full-time job as books editor at AOL. Many of you in the Manhattan media world first met me then, spending half of each week in New York. It wasn't easy, with two young daughters at home, but it had its moments, and for all who helped me during those years, much gratitude.

After AOL came quite a few jobs I'd rather forget for various reasons, but I'd like to thank a few individuals from along the way: Sarah Nelson at *Publishers Weekly*, now an editor at Harper-Collins. Jim Milliot at *Publishers Weekly* (and thanks for the current work, sir!). Robin Lenz at Shelf Awareness (hope Florida is treating you well). Paul O'Donnell of *Washingtonian* magazine. Rob Irvine of Perfect Sense/Brightspot. Kristen Shaughnessy and Matt Besterman at NY1. The TV crew of WETA-PBS who filmed *The Book Studio* from 2007 to 2010, not to mention the incredible authors and publicists I worked with on that show (special shout-out to Paul Peachey of Bookfame who brought so many big names down to the WETA offices: "Just past the Weenie-Beanie . . .").

After AOL also came Twitter. Many of you know me from my tweets alone, even if you've met me in real life (IRL). Because I tweeted like crazy for a couple of years I was fortunate to amass a large following and introduce a hashtag, #FridayReads. Thanks to each and every one of you who has followed me, read my tweets, and/or shared your #FridayReads over the past fifteen years. It has been a wild, unexpected, and mostly glorious ride. I'm not sure if I could do justice to my Twitter experience if I named any one of you, so please allow me instead to share my memories of Lisa Bonchek Adams, a talented writer, devoted friend, and all-around beautiful human being who died of metastatic breast cancer in 2013. Twitter hasn't been and can never be the same without Lisa's presence. I would like to extend my continued sympathies and love to her family: her husband Clarke, and their children, Paige, Colin, and Tristan.

————

As I tweeted, I also wrote, mostly book reviews, author profiles, and the like.

Enormous thanks to my onetime editor and longtime friend Ron Charles, fiction critic at *The Washington Post*. We're overdue for a meal made entirely out of cake and pastry, Ron.

Thanks to Laurie Hertzel, the inimitable books editor at the Minneapolis *StarTribune*.

Thanks also to Stephanie Merry, my editor at *The Washington Post* for several years, and Nora Krug, her fellow editor, and Becky Meloan, assistant editor.

Thanks to Lucy Feldman, books and culture editor at *Time* magazine.

Thanks to Kate Tuttle who, as interim books editor at *The Boston Globe*, ran my reviews—she's now the books editor at *People* magazine, congrats!

Thanks to Tom Beer, once of *Newsday*, now editor in chief of *Kirkus Reviews*.

Thanks to Allan Fallow and Christina Ianzito of *AARP: The Magazine*.

Thanks to Jonny Diamond and Emily Firetog of *Literary Hub*.

Thanks to Anita Felicelli of *Alta*'s California Book Club.

Thanks to Emma Sarappo at *The Atlantic* books section, and her editors and fact-checkers.

Huge thanks to Boris Kachka at the *Los Angeles Times*, and onward!

Thanks to Barbara Brownell Grogan, Susan Straight, Susan Tyler Hitchcock, and Sanaa Akach (among others) at National Geographic Books.

Thanks to Lucas Wittmann and Ron Hogan at Regan Arts/ Phaidon, as well as the late Gregory Henry.

My life took a turn in 2021 when Jeff Umbro of the Podglomerate hired me to host and produce a new podcast called *Missing Pages* about scams and scandals in the publishing industry. Thank you, Jeff, and thank you to the amazing team: Caila Litman, Jordan Aaron, Matt Keeley, Chris Boniello, Joni Deutsch, Madison

Richards, Morgan Swift, and Dan Christo. So glad we're continuing with season two.

———

Friendship with other writers is essential to this work.

Thank you, Karen Palmer, for the Twitter friendship, the IRL friendship, for hosting me in Los Angeles, for meeting me in DC, for the high-level book talk, the support, the wisdom, the care.

Never-ending thanks to Sarah Sandman, of Purdue University Fort Wayne, for friendship, laughs, and a lot of deep work on this book.

Teresa Henderson, you are precious to me. Thanks for the biscotti alle mandorle and your patience!

Lorraine Berry, when they say "you haven't yet met all the people who are going to love you," they're talking about you.

Susan Coll and Paul Goldberg, for beta reading (Susan) and the best flavored vodkas (Paul).

Louis Bayard, for liquid lunches and more.

Mary Kay Zuravleff, who believes in my as-yet-unpublished novel.

Dani Shapiro and Michael Maren, who inspire me in so many ways.

Betsy Andrews and mes soeurs de Plascassier, who inspired me to continue processing trauma (but not because they were traumatic! What a week in Provence that was . . .)

Lily Burana and family, a safe harbor emotionally, mentally, and physically. To our milspouse Cosa Nostra!

Chris Bohjalian—you've really helped me. Thank you so much.

Robert Rorke, from shared LRBs to shared submission trauma, I salute you.

Michiko Clark, from the Blue Lagoon to the Brooklyn Botanic Garden. What's next?

To all my PEN/Faulkner colleagues, including Gwydion

Suilebhan, Lacey Dunham, Shahenda Helmy (now of The Loft in Minneapolis!)

The Wednesday Night Writers Club: You know who you are. Special mention to the divine Brenda Copeland and how easily she's managed to make me want to move to Washington Heights.

To Melissa Scholes-Young, you know what for . . . and can't wait for our next Millie's lunch.

———

Other friends:

Sarah Wright and George French.

James and Julia Cricks.

Erik Kulleseid and Mark Eisenhardt.

Susan and Anthony Acquisto.

Patricia Lopez Blickstein.

Phyllis Crowder Carr.

Robin Noonan and Tom Lovett.

Dori Vallone and Chris Phillips.

Deborah Wilson.

Elisabeth Prueitt.

Mike and Rita Bacon.

Eleanor Pryor.

Kara Chiles and Ian Little.

Suzanne and Tom Gainey.

Ian and Rosalind Cameron-Mowat.

Kathy McCabe.

Barbara Benham.

Cynthia Szabo Yousef.

Holly Johnson Stuhr.

Jenny Gillis.

Maddy John Bacher.

Bernadette and Michelle Humphrey-Nicol.

Anne Leonhardt.

Kimberly Noake MacPhee.

Susan Stang.

Melanie Holcomb.

Roger and Adrienne Tufts.

Madeleine McAllister.

Tom and Nicola Noll.

Gloria Freund.

Barbara Garren.

Jan Dabrowski.

Becky and Tim Poe.

Tony Poole.

———

Two important in memoriam mentions:

To FBR, for our spiritual connection.

To CMC, for over three decades of love, and for sharing your birthday with my first child.

———

Last, but far from least, my family.

To my late father: thank you for being my number-one fan and a great example of kindness.

To my mother: thank you for all your love and support, but especially thank you for reading to me so early and so often.

To my sister: on to our futures.

To our daughters: I love you. Full stop.

To my husband: my OAO.

BETHANNE PATRICK maintains a storied place in the publishing industry as a critic and as @TheBookMaven on Twitter, where she created the popular #FridayReads and regularly comments on books and literary ideas to over 200,000 followers. Her work appears frequently in the *Los Angeles Times* as well as at *The Washington Post*, NPR Books, and *Literary Hub*. She sits on the board of the PEN/Faulkner Foundation and has served on the board of the National Book Critics Circle. She is the host of the *Missing Pages* podcast. Find out more at bethannepatrick.com.